AF141330

NICHOLAS W. BALABKINS

Not by Theory alone...

Volkswirtschaftliche Schriften

Begründet von Prof. Dr. Dr. h.c. J. Broermann

Heft 382

Not by Theory alone...

The Economics of Gustav von Schmoller and Its Legacy to America

Von

Prof. Nicholas W. Balabkins

Duncker & Humblot / Berlin

CIP-Titelaufnahme der Deutschen Bibliothek

Balabkins, Nicholas W.:
Not by theory alone... : the economics of Gustav von
Schmoller and its legacy to America / von Nicholas W.
Balabkins. - Berlin : Duncker u. Humblot, 1988
(Volkswirtschaftliche Schriften ; H. 382)
ISBN 3-428-06450-X
NE: GT

Alle Rechte vorbehalten
© 1988 Duncker & Humblot GmbH, Berlin 41
Satz: Hagedornsatz, Berlin 46
Druck: Berliner Buchdruckerei Union GmbH, Berlin 61
Printed in Germany
ISBN 3-428-06450-X

Preface

Anybody who is invited to read a book like this one has a right to know what it is about and what reading it would be good for. While this is true for any book, a word of explanation is imperative in the case of this work. Gustav Schmoller, who was born more than a hundredandfifty years ago, is ignored by professional economists today. The few who know about him generally consider his work irrelevant. Yet it is unclear what this implicit judgement could be based on. When we come across a reference to Schmoller, the information it contains is generally either totally misleading or outright wrong. In his time, Schmoller was one of the most respected professional economists in the world, working in one of the leading research universities in a country blessed with innovative and prospering industries and a political system that, despite its obvious anachronisms, had produced the most advanced welfare legislation. Schmoller's ambition was to make economics interesting and relevant, useful for practical purposes in politics and business, and he was therefore critical of the received university doctrines in economics. As Marshall, in Cambridge, who shared his concerns, he tried to reorient the economics profession from within with new approaches to research and instruction. Today, economics has lost most of its appeal to those Schmoller was able to attract. Future public administrators will rather turn to law, management or computer science than economics. Future business leaders will study management, marketing and finance, but not economics. A thorough understanding of the economy is widely considered irrelevant for success as a professional economist. Schmoller's ambitions and concerns are shared by many today. Few know about his program, how he launched it and how it fared. This book gives an introduction to Schmoller and his work and its significance to American economics. The book is designed as the road-map for those who want to travel in the vast and unknown territory of Schmoller's detailed studies of the development of economic institutions and their effect upon economic activity.

Schmoller's program was aptly described by Joseph Alois Schumpeter in his 1926 article.[1] Since that article is not available in English, let me quote and translate:

> "If you want to understand the specific situation in which a particular economy happens to be at a certain time, and if you want to suggest something relevant about its current problems, then everything that in theoretical economics is taken as given, assumed to be invariant and ignored in the course of analysis becomes the main subject of investigation

---

[1] Joseph A. Schumpeter, "Gustav von Schmoller und die Probleme von heute", *Schmollers Jahrbuch für Gesetzgebung, Verwaltung und Volkswirtschaft* 50, 1926, pp. 373-388 (1-52).

and focal point of interest. These data include the particulars of a nation's economic environment, the endowment with natural resources, capital and machinery, the position in international trade, the social structure, size, composition and distribution of the social product, and the economic and political constitution. In this case, the collection of facts and figures becomes the paramount task, completion of which is a precondition for further research. The second task is to put all this information together in a definite order, in order to make it accessible. Once these two steps have been made, a number of important questions are ready to be answered. The first and the second task can never be quite completed, work on them progresses as the available material is being used and as new methods are developed for data collection and use. Soon, there arises a need to analyse the technical relationships, the real behaviour of social groups and individuals, the constitution and functioning of social institutions such as the state, property, commercial law, etc. The sum of these analyses forms the sociological and economic knowledge of a period, and one can try to forge this knowledge together into a provisional synthesis. It is important to note that Schmoller has actually worked his way through all the stages of this program, and therein lies his greatness." (pp. 17-18)

Later in the same essay, Schumpeter offers a different characterization. The Schmoller program consisted in "approaching the material with a minimum burden of a priori, thereby capturing interdependencies which enter as additional a priori; this yields the (provisional) framework for investigation, a framework that is further refined in a continuing interplay of subject matter and mental process. That this program could once be regarded as specific to a particular school is evidence for the importance of the task Schmoller confronted; that the program is commonplace today underscores Schmoller's success." (pp. 45-46)

It is well known, and Professor Balabkins stresses the point on several occasions, that Schmoller tended to address not only questions of "is" but also of "ought". He was not content with an analysis that did not point the way towards the successful solution of a practical problem. The approach has puzzled many critics, who used to a strict distinction between positive and normative economics, tend to think that a combination of both is methodologically inadmissible. As a matter of fact, Schmoller's "oughts" are not the "oughts" of welfare economics. He arrives at policy prescriptions by enriching the analysis sufficiently with historical, institutional, political, fiscal, and cultural data such as to impose constraints on the set of available solutions. In the end, the choice range for economic policy has been effectively narrowed down, not by means of normative judgement but rather through a process of institutionally rich analysis. As the following discussion by Schumpeter shows, Schmoller's political economy not only differs from contemporary economics by method, but more importantly by subject matter.

"Almost generally accepted is the fact that there are moments of social and political crisis in which the political interests of classes and parties largely coincide — we think of the analogy of a sinking ship.

More important, but not quite as generally accepted is the other fact that political parties of differing programs, once in power, in normal times cannot engage in radically different policies. Not only will they discharge their routine duties in more or less the same way, even the far-reaching political decisions which mark an entire period are taken quite irrespective of the color of the party currently in power. (pp. 8-9)

Once we have acknowledged these premises, one of the reasons for the supposed impossibility of a nation's common policy objective at a particular time is no longer valid.

The policy measure that needs to be taken now is determined by the necessities of the moment. It corresponds to a situation inherited from the immediate past. The basic facts are given and cannot be readily changed. What is generally considered a policy issue needs a political response, what is widely considered as critical or dangerous needs to be avoided, what is widely considered desirable needs to be attained. What has been begun needs to be continued or brought to an orderly completion. Questions that have been raised cannot be ignored. Therefore both the elected politician as an individual as well as the elected group or party are embedded in a system of given circumstances, necessities and responsibilities that do not leave them a choice between an infinite number of options, nor allow them the luxury to pursue those policies which directly follow from their ideological predispositions. Where this is ignored, failure and defeat loom immediately." (pp. 9-10)

Schmoller's "oughts" can be interpreted as the results of an approach to political economy that proceeds by enriching the analysis with qualitative and quantitative data until the set of solutions has been narrowly constrained.

When Schmoller emphasizes the need for a normative or policy-oriented approach to economics, his intention is not to make economic analysis subservient to his own private political opinions. He did not disagree with Max Weber and his followers on the need to separate personal convictions from scholarly analysis. He did, however, teach that values are important in economic activity, and in particular in political economy. Hence, the kind of economic knowledge we can produce in political economy, in his own words, is composed of intellectual understanding and practical purpose, where ultimately the purpose has to guide the intellectual endeavour. From there it follows that economic theories are important tools, not ends in themselves. Although Schmoller was by no means uninterested in theory and kept up with theoretical developments in economics in both the German language and international academic journals until his death, he was consistently critical of theorizing that could not conceivably serve a practical purpose. This theme is developed in the sixth chapter of the present book.

Many have found Schmoller's work inaccessible, found the material presented overwhelming and deplored a lack of structure and sharp contours. Zimmermann[2], a student of Schmollers, describes how this feeling was shared among many young economists who came to his lectures, himself included. Schmoller's

---

[2] Waldemar Zimmermann, "Gustav von Schmoller und der akademische Nachwuchs", in Arthur Spiethof (ed.) *Gustav von Schmoller und die deutsche geschichtliche Volkswirt-schaftslehre*, Festgabe zur hundertsten Wiederkehr seines Geburtstages 24. 6. 1938, Berlin: Duncker & Humblot, 1938, pp. 349-364 (360).

theories were not built on the principles of elegance and parsimony, as contemporary economic theories are. Schmoller was interested in developing theoretical constructions which were fit to capture an economic phenomenon in its historical dimension, theoretical structures that at the same time, apart from the economic essence, could also accommodate the relevant historical, sociological and political theories and facts bearing upon the economic phenomenon. Why did he not confine himself to a simple underlying structure around which to build his principles of historical economics and thus make it easier for economists to learn from him and perhaps subscribe to his views? The reason is readily explained. Schmoller did not primarily want to succeed with his students or his fellow economists. He wanted to train able civil servants who, on the basis of a thorough education in all the relevant areas of public administration, would be reluctant to superimpose predetermined views on complex situations. Numerous offers to write the authoritative principles of economics he declined. Rather, in almost fifty years of writing, rewriting, researching and re-researching he developed what he modestly called the basic outline (Grundriss) of comprehensive, institutionally rich, and practically relevant political economy. Schmoller attached great importance to this work. After retiring from active teaching duties (at the age of 75), he devoted the last five years of his life to prepare a second thoroughly revised edition and saw to its completion.

Unfortunate labels can deter serious study just as much as complex theoretical concepts. The attribute "historical" suggests that the approach is a thing of the past in more than one sense. Yet an institutionally rich political economy can forego the prodigious use of historical research just as little as theoretical physics the use of mathematical analysis. This reliance does not reduce theoretical physics to bad mathematics nor Schmoller's economics to bad history. An institutionally rich and practically realistic political economy can hardly be expected to thrive if it is reduced to the use of one methodology at the expense of the other. A balance of different methods, not the exclusive use of one over the other was what Schmoller stood for.

While Schmoller's program has survived and is well in academia, notably in America, his name is remembered by very few, but his work remains thoroughly inaccessible. In the economics discipline, the institutionalist approach has some of its roots in Schmoller's approach. Economics as a professional discipline, however, has lost its prominence side by side with the law schools. Business schools and schools of public administration continue the emphasis on institutionally rich, theoretically sound and multidisciplinary scholarship that can lead to practical solutions. Perhaps it is time that economics need not be sterile and unrealistic. Perhaps it is time to insist on its usefulness. And perhaps this book can help bring about the reconsideration of a man's work who stood for those practical values.

Maastricht, February 8, 1988

Prof. Dr. Jürgen Backhaus
Rijksuniversiteit Limburg

Inhaltsverzeichnis

Chapter I

Schmoller: Street-Smart Years

Gustav Schmoller was born on June 24, 1838, in Heilbronn, north of the modern city of Stuttgart, in what today is the state of Baden-Württemberg, one of the eleven constituent states of the Federal Republic of Germany. He died on June 27, 1917, in Bad Harzburg.[1] His mother, nee Therese Gärtner, came from Calw, a small industrial town in Württemberg, known in the 17th and 18th centuries for its cloth industry. In her ancestry were physicians and well-known scholars in the natural sciences.[2] His father, Ludwig Friedrich David Schmoller was born in 1795, became a soldier in 1813, and saw combat duty against the armies of Napoleon. He rose to the rank of an officer and was seriously wounded in battle. He was knighted for his services to the royal house of Württemberg, and he died in 1865 in Heilbronn. The ancestral family may have originated in Russia, for, according to Schmoller's own interpretation, the name Schmoller is supposedly a Slavonic word and refers to 'smoller', meaning a charcoal burner.[3] Schmoller's friend and supporter in Halle, Heinrich Leo, had forever repeated this tale.[4]

Schmoller's father was a business administrator of the royal estates of Württemberg, so the young Schmoller grew up in a materially comfortable home. His father's house was large and well appointed, with a beautiful garden-full of fruit trees and flowers. Located in the center of the town, its spacious courtyard and garden served the children as a playground.[5] Schmoller lost his mother when he was nine years old, so he was actually brought up by his father. According to Schmoller, his father was an industrious and forceful personality with a sunny disposition.[6] Even though his father worked long hours in the

---

[1] Meitzel, C., "Schmoller, Gustav v.," in *Handwörterbuch der Staatswissenschaften*, Jena, Fischer, 1926, vol. 7, pp. 251-253.

[2] Schmoller, G., "Meine Heilbronner Jugendjahre," in *Von schwäbischer Scholle*, Heilbronn, Verlag Eugen Salzer, 1918, p. 55.

[3] *Smolitj* in Russian means to tar or to apply pitch. It could very well be that Schmoller's friend, who told him the supposed origin of the name, could have referred to the Russian word *smoljar* or even more properly *smoliljschchik*, somebody who applies pitch.

[4] n.a. *Reden und Ansprachen gehalten am 24. Juni 1908 bei der Feier von Gustav Schmollers 70. Geburtstag*, Altenburg, 1908, p. 47.

[5] Schmoller, G., *op. cit.*, p. 53.

[6] *Ibid.*, p. 54.

office, he maintained a light touch, so to speak. He strove to educate his children by example and admonition; he stressed the importance of continuous application on their part, for otherwise they would amount to nothing in life.[7] His accounts of his wartime experiences left a profound impression upon the children.[8]

From early childhood, Schmoller learned to understand and appreciate the needs, wants, and living conditions of ordinary folk. In his father's business office he regularly met people from all walks of life, be they workers or farmers. These daily contacts gave him an early insight into the nature of the prevailing social and economic institutions, the process of legislation, and the administrative practices of the small kingdom. He also spent his summer vacations with his grandparents in Calw, which at that time was one of the most industrial towns in Württemberg. In Calw, he came to know well the prevailing life styles and living conditions of the industrial workers, craftsmen, peasants, businessmen, and government officials. All these early experiences must have left an indelible impression upon the young Schmoller.[9]

Schmoller Sr. wanted Gustav to become a civil servant like himself. Although Gustav's junior academic high school years were boring, as he claimed at the end of his life, his senior high school was more taxing and stimulating. He took his high school diploma in the spring of 1856, third in his class.[10] Upon graduation, on account of his delicate health, Schmoller Sr. urged his son to skip a year and a half and spend it in his office to get even better acquainted with the administrative problems of the royal government and household.[11] The young man obliged, and during 1856-57 he learned the financial and administrative practices of his native Württemberg. He also travelled and became familiar with the lay of the land, its roads, rivers, bridges and the numerous customs houses as well. But above all, he observed life at the grassroots and acquainted himself with the prevailing economic and social conditions.[12]

Prior to working with his father, Schmoller took private lessons in higher mathematics for a few months with a certain Mr. Riekher. But, as Schmoller wrote at the very end of his life, it was this early experience with his father that

---

[7] *Ibid.*, p. 55.

[8] n.a., *Reden und Ansprachen gehalten am 24. Juni 1908 bei der Feier von Gustav Schmollers 70. Geburtstag*, Altenburg, 1908, p. 48.

[9] Francke, E., "Gustav Schmoller und die Sozialreform," in *Soziale Praxis und Archiv für Volkswohlfahrt*, vol. 26, # 44, 1917, p. 862.

[10] Schmoller, G., *Meine Heilbronner Jugendjahre*, p. 54. See also, *Reden und Ansprachen*, p. 48.

[11] Hintze, O., "Schmoller, Gustav v.," in *Deutsches Biographisches Jahrbuch. Überleitungsband II: 1917-1920*, Stuttgart, 1928, p. 125.

[12] Hintze, O., Spiethoff, A., Beckerath, E. v., "Gustav von Schmoller, 1838-1917," in *Lebensbilder grosser Nationalökonomen*, edited by Horst C. Recktenwald, Köln and Berlin, Kiepenheuer und Witsch, 1965, p. 334.

laid a foundation for his subsequent development and interests. This early practical knowledge of life, something that today we might call being street-smart, shaped his intellectual development and perceptions of reality.[13] Throughout his life, Schmoller's thinking, judgement, and inferences were based on real-life experiences and perceptions of social and economic problems — not on neat abstract, logical and simplified constructions of reality. To paraphrase Schmoller, one could probably lay down his maxim as follows:

"Grass-roots experience is a great asset; it enables you to recognize a mistake every time you repeat it!"

In October 1857, Schmoller enrolled at the University of Tübingen to major in *Kameralwissenschaft*,[14] a term which in America has been described as a discipline "which combines public finance, statistics, economics, administrative science, history and even sociology."[15] From today's mainstream perspective, such a major is nonsensical. Was this *Kameralwissenschaft* a field of inquiry which turned a young man into a jack-of-all-trades and master of none?

What is almost always forgotten today, particularly by English-speaking economists, is that for centuries Germany, like Italy, was but a geographic concept. In reality, Germany consisted of some 300 German-speaking kingdoms, duchies, free cities, and tiny principalities. These political entities were forever threatened by their stronger neighbors. To assure their continued survival, these small states, each headed by an aristocrat, developed strong bureaucracies, run by officials trained in all aspects of statecraft. As a rule they were graduates with a degree in *Kameralwissenschaft*. The object of this science was to teach future government officials "how to preserve and increase the general means" of the state.[16] It taught them how to maintain law and order, how to keep the roads, bridges, and watermains in good repair, how to improve nutrition, and how to cultivate lands properly.[17] In other words, it was a hands-on training for the solution of the pressing social and economic problems, designed to preserve the survival of one of the 300 small, but sovereign German-speaking entities. It was only after the end of the Napoleonic wars when, by 1815, the number had been reduced to 38.

Schmoller pursued his studies with gusto; he was an eager beaver. He strove to obtain as broad an education as possible, but his economics preparation got

---

[13] *Reden und Ansprachen*, p. 49; see also, Schmoller's *Meine Heilbronner Jugendjahre*, p. 57.

[14] Schmoller, G., "Meine Heilbronner Jugendjahre," in *Von schwäbischer Scholle*, Heilbronn, Verlag Eugen Salzer, 1918, p. 54.

[15] Fischer, W., "Schmoller, Gustav," in *International Encyclopedia of the Social Sciences*, vol. 14, New York, The Macmillan Company and The Free Press, 1968, p. 60.

[16] Small, A. W., *The Camarelists. The Pioneers of German Social Polity*, Chicago, The University of Chicago Press, 1909, p. 441.

[17] *Ibid.*, pp. 442-444.

short shrift, according to his own admission.[18] He diligently attended classes in philosophy and history, as well as in chemistry, physics, mechanics, and technology. Even as a student he quietly hoped that one day he would be able to embark upon an academic career; that is, to teach at a university.[19] Schmoller's 'delicate health' dictated that he abstain from such time-honored student pastimes as duelling, beer drinking, and active fraternity life. Student Schmoller had no use for the *Burschenschaften*. As semesters went by, the young man became more erudite, and he felt particularly drawn to the study of history.

Deep in his heart was a wish to become an academic. He was not exactly precocious, but neither was he a late bloomer, and he felt that the time had come to speak his mind. He decided to take part in an essay prize contest which dealt with the economic ideas of the Reformation. He won the gold medal,[20] and his essay was published in the *Tübinger Zeitschrift*.[21] In Tübingen Schmoller acquired a lifelong love for history. Presumably, while still a student, he started to use history for the purposes of making the study of economics more empirical. At Tübingen, as in other German universities, the "laissez-faire" economic philosophy was quite strong and widely accepted, even though some German economists like Wilhelm Roscher, Bruno Hildebrand and Karl Knies, had already raised considerable doubts about its claim of universal applicability. Slowly that outcry against the English classical school of economics, known as "Manchestertum," which signified the advocacy of unrestricted individual freedom from government intervention in industry and trade, became known as the German Historical School of Economics. At that time, however, Schmoller was still a captive of a classical school of economics.

He was graduated in the summer of 1861 after passing 'the first cameral exam,' in German known as "das erste kameralistische Examen."[22] Shortly thereafter, he took his doctorate as well.[23] But Schmoller still had to pass the 'second exam,' known as 'zweites Staatsexamen.' To prepare himself adequately for it, Schmoller was required to discharge his 'clerkship' duty by spending a prescribed number of months at some lower level government office, and, thereafter, a few more months at the central royal administrative offices of the Kingdom of Württemberg. He spent the first part of the clerkship in his father's office in Heilbronn, where he had worked before. Since he already knew

---

[18] *Reden und Ansprachen*, p. 49. See also, Schmoller's *Meine Heilbronner Jugendjahre*, p. 59.

[19] Schmoller, G., "Meine Heilbronner Jugendjahre," in *Von schwäbischer Scholle*, Heilbronn, Verlag Eugen Salzer, 1918, p. 59.

[20] *Ibid.*, p. 60.

[21] Hintze, O., "Schmoller, Gustav v.," in *Deutsches Biographisches Jahrbuch. Überleitungsband II: 1917-1920*, Stuttgart, 1928, p. 125.

[22] Schmoller, G., "Meine Heilbronner Jugendjahre," in *Von schwäbischer Scholle*, Heilbronn, Verlag Eugen Salzer, 1918, p. 60.

[23] Hintze, O., Spiethoff, A., Beckerath, E. v., "Gustav von Schmoller (1838-1917)," in *op. cit.*, p. 334.

intimately the administrative business, his father permitted him to devote all his time to reading. He read voraciously the works of the German philosophers during this interlude. In keeping with the family's tradition, the young man wanted to be qualified for a possible career in the bureaucracy of his native Württemberg, but all these plans came to nothing.

The second part of his clerkship turned out to be of immense significance for Schmoller's subsequent career and life. Schmoller passed both examinations with 'distinction.'[24] It so happened that his brother-in-law, Gustav Rümelin, who also hailed from Heilbronn, was in charge of the Statistical Office of Württemberg. He asked the young Schmoller to analyze and evaluate the State's industrial craft census of 1861.[25] Schmoller spent the entire summer of 1862 in Stuttgart on this job.[26] The fruits of his first major venture into statistics were published in 1862 in *Württemberg's* Yearbook. At about the same time, the self-confident young man rashly published an anonymous brochure in which he analyzed the Prussian-French trade treaty of 1861. He made no bones about his Prussian sympathies at the expense of Austria on whose side stood Württemberg. Even though Schmoller thought that no one would ever discover the identity of the author, it turned out differently.[27] At the end of his life, Schmoller recalled how his father entered the room, pale as a ghost, saying: "There you have it; it's written in the paper that you are the real author of this brochure. From now on any career in Württemberg for you is out of the question."[28]

Whatever ambitions the young man had for a bureaucratic career in Württemberg crumbled into dust. He had to re-orient himself, to shift gears, to look for a different way of making a living. Fortunately, Schmoller was not destitute, and he could afford to take his time. From 1862 through 1864, he was intensely preoccupied with the relationship between ethics and methodology and their possible impact on economics. The young Schmoller in his mid-twenties was already thinking and tackling 'big' issues in the social sciences. At that time, methodologically speaking, he was a veritable captive of the philosophers Kant and Schopenhauer, and Rümelin, his brother-in-law, as he admitted in 1911.[29] He never finished the manuscript he wrote on this topic, and Schmoller was glad for that.

---

[24] *Reden und Ansprachen ...*, p. 50.

[25] Hintze, O., "Schmoller, Gustav v.," in *Deutsches Biographisches Jahrbuch: Überleitungsband II: 1917-1920*, Stuttgart, 1928, p. 126.

[26] Schmoller, *op. cit.*, p. 60.

[27] Skalweit, A., "Vorwort des Herausgebers," in Gustav von Schmoller, *Die Volkswirtschaft, die Volkswirtschaftslehre und ihre Methode, 1893*, Frankfurt am Main, Vittorio Klostermann, 1949, p. 3.

[28] Schmoller, G., *Meine Heilbronner Jugendjahre*, p. 61. See also, *Reden und Ansprachen ...*, p. 50.

[29] Schmoller, G., "Volkswirtschaft, Volkswirtschaftslehre und -methode," in *Handwörterbuch der Staatswissenschaften*, vol. 8, Jena, G. Fischer, 1911, p. 426.

Thus, at the age of 24, he had completed his higher education and had gained considerable administrative experience. By that time he had already developed a certain streak of intellectual independence and stubbornness, and he knew that economics was a field of knowledge which "cannot be separated from space, time, and nationality, and whose foundations ... were to be sought not alone, but primarily in history."[30] During this period of uncertainty, the young man did not despair. In 1863, he spent the summer months in Geneva, Switzerland, where he polished his French. In his old age, he recalled that upon his return from Geneva in the fall of that year, he even dreamt in French.[31] In the spring of 1864, Schmoller made a rather extensive trip visiting Germany's well-known university towns, such as Heidelberg, Frankfurt am Main, Würzburg, Leipzig, Marburg, Göttingen, Hamburg, and Berlin, hoping for a job offer. While in Berlin, he got a job offer from the University of Halle.

---

[30] Anderson, P. R., "Gustav von Schmoller (1838-1917)," in *Essays in Modern European Historiography*, edited and with an Introduction by S. William Halperin, Chicago and London, The University of Chicago Press, 1971, p. 293.

[31] Schmoller, G., *Meine Heilbronner Jugendjahre*, p. 61.

Chapter II

"Not by Economic Theory Alone ..."

"Man proposes, God disposes," says an old proverb. The jobless Schmoller never dreamed that an academic job was just around the corner. His analysis of the 1861 census of Württemberg, published in 1862, had fallen into the hands of Herr von Beuermann, the Kurator (the counterpart of the present-day Provost) of the University of Halle, located today in the German Democratic Republic (East Germany). Von Beuermann very much liked Schmoller's statistical, policy-oriented work and recommended that the young scholar be invited to teach at Halle.[1] Schmoller accepted at once and became an Associate Professor of Economics at an annual salary of only 500 Reichstaler.[2] The following year, he was offered a job at the University of Zürich. He did not accept it, but was able to use the offer to gain promotion to full professor at Halle.[3] Schmoller succeeded Professor Johann Friedrich Gottfried Eiselen, who had taught primarily the economy, administration, and law of Prussia.[4] Schmoller knew little about that subject; indeed, he felt he had 'no ground under his feet in the state of Prussia,' because he was not familiar with its history, constitution, or administration.[5] By contrast, he felt at home with the economy, history, and administration of Württemberg, his native state, because he had learned the intimate details of all three while working for his father. Thus, as he confessed at the celebration of his 70th birthday, it was in Halle where Schmoller realized that one cannot judge properly and evaluate economic and social problems without an adequate knowledge of the entire administrative apparatus of the government. It was indispensable to know the many details of how the huge governmental machine runs, what it influences, and what it is influenced by. Since Schmoller did not have the opportunity to learn these administrative details the way he had learned them in his father's office in Württemberg, he decided to study on his own the law, administration, and history of Prussia.[6] In this manner he developed his

---

[1] Schmoller, G., "Meine Heilbronner Jugendjahre," in *Von schwäbischer Scholle*, Heilbronn, Verlag Eugen Salzer, 1918, p. 61.

[2] n. a., *Reden und Ansprachen gehalten am 24. Juni bei der Feier von Gustav Schmollers 70. Geburtstag*, Altenburg, 1908, p. 50.

[3] Meitzel, C., "Schmoller, G. v.," in *Handwörterbuch der Staatswissenschaften*, vol. 7, Jena, Gustav Fischer, 1926, p. 251.

[4] Hintze, O., "Schmoller, Gustav v.," in *Deutsches Biographisches Jahrbuch. Überleitungsband II: 1917-1920*, Stuttgart, 1928, p. 126.

[5] *Reden und Ansprachen gehalten am 24. Juni bei der Feier von Gustav Schmollers 70. Geburtstag*, Altenburg, 1908, p. 51.

[6] *Reden und Ansprachen gehalten am 24. Juni bei der Feier von Gustav Schmollers 70. Geburtstag*, Altenburg, 1908, p. 52.

unique tie between economics and historical research. Even at this early stage of his academic career, Schmoller disliked pure deductive theory. He had too many interests. His model was his brother-in-law Rümelin, who preached that it was better to be a universally educated man than to be a pure specialist who knows everything about nothing, as we would say today. This tendency of Schmoller's is probably the reason why some specialists have dubbed him a diletante.

Soon after his arrival at Halle, Schmoller became a town councilor, a position he held from 1864 to 1872.[7] As councilor, he would later say, he gained considerable practical experience and understanding of how a big town runs and what makes it tick. He learned all the fascinating details of the constitutional life of a city. The experience enabled him, during the 1869-1880 period, to turn to serious study of the economic history of various cities.[8] It also led him to base his thinking on living and on personal experiences, and not just on abstract and logical concepts.

In Halle, the young professor also married Lucie Rathgen, the daughter of a high government official from Weimar. He described his wife as a "herrliches Weib," which in English would mean a 'magnificent woman.'[9]

Since Halle was quite close to Berlin, he went there often and occasionally he visited the Statistical Office, headed by Ernst Engels.[10] The library of the Statistical Office had a good collection of books and periodicals which Schmoller diligently examined. However, the major attraction for Schmoller was the office's archives on Kloster Street, where he pored over an incredible number of files. He was determined to save from obscurity the Prussian king, Friedrich Wilhelm I, the father of Friedrich the Great. At that time, Friedrich Wilhelm I was considered to have been a little more than an admirer of his tall soldiers and the founder of an orderly administration, but otherwise nobody had really examined his legacy.

Schmoller spent probably two decades studying Friedrich and wrote numerous articles.[11] He was particularly interested in the king's administrative practices, legal institutions, and financial policies between 1688 and 1740. Prussia's meteoric rise among the European powers, already one of Schmoller's many interests, now became an intellectual obsession for him. During this time, the young academic led a busy life in Halle caught up in classroom work, seminars, service as a town councilor, the demands of two children, and, of

---

[7] Schmoller, G., *Deutsches Städtewesen in älterer Zeit*, Aalen, Scientia Verlag, 1964. Reprint of 1922 edition, p. IV.

[8] Schmoller, G., "Meine Heilbronner Jugendjahre'" in *Von schwäbischer Scholle*, Heilbronn, Verlag Eugen Salzer, 1918, p. 57.

[9] *Ibid.*, p. 61. See also *Reden und Ansprachen gehalten am 24 Juni bei der Feier von Gustav Schmollers 70. Geburtstag*, Altenburg, 1908, p. 53.

[10] Knapp, G. F., *Einführung in einige Hauptgebiete der Nationalökonomie*, München, Verlag Duncker und Humblot, 1925, p. 363.

[11] *Ibid.*, p. 363.

course, research and writing. For Schmoller research and teaching were always closely intertwined. In this period, he wrote a series of articles on many different subjects, showing his wide intellectual interests. For instance, he published an article on the economic and social conditions of the United States after the Civil War. Another field of interest to Schmoller was the history over several centuries of meat consumption and cattle and meat prices in Germany. Sheep-farming, wool prices, and statistics on sheep were another field of interest.[12] Already at this time, the salient feature of Schmoller's scholarship was his emphasis on history and social statistics as a source of information. The major work that emerged during his years at Halle was *Zur Geschichte der deutschen Klein-gewerbe im 19. Jahrhundert. Statistische und nationalökonomische Untersuchun-gen* (704 pages), published in 1870. *Zur Geschichte*, Schmoller's first major monograph, deals with the evolution of German small-scale industry and crafts in the nineteenth century and shows the scope of Schmoller's research interests. Since nobody reads this work nowadays, permit me to give the reader some of its flavor.[13] Schmoller first describes the ravages of the Thirty-Year War (1618-1648) on the German territory. Because at that time Germany was a geographic concept, not a unified country (it consisted of three hundred 'little' Germanies, a situation called 'Kleinstaatlerei'), there was little possibility for speedy recovery and reconstruction. Stagnation and retrogression were the inevitable result (p. 16). Schmoller, who had a lifelong interest in things Prussian, details how the Prussian kings purposefully encouraged the immigration of Dutch and French craftsmen in 1667, in 1669, and in 1683 in order to stimulate the development of crafts and industry (p. 24). The Prussian government also used a strong hand to cope with the restrictive trade and craft policies of the guilds (p. 27). Friedrich the Great, for example, established one hundred villages and brought in foreign expertise and the latest technology. The Prussian government encouraged, stimulated, and guided Prussia's business community (p. 30). Private ownership of the means of production was the rule, not the exception.

Between 1784 und 1847 the growth of Prussia's crafts was quite impressive. Schmoller assembled exhaustive data on the number of master-craftsmen in 1784 and 1847. Then he calculated the ratio of people to master-craftsmen in those two bench-mark years. For instance, in 1784 Prussia had 269 master-carpenters or 417 people per one master-carpenter. In 1847, 2,208 master-carpenters were in existence, or 185 Prussians per master-craftsman. From such numbers Schmoller made his inferences about Prussia's structural change and economic growth (p. 36). He made the following observations to the laissez-faire pundits: 'If you believe that Prussian crafts could have developed more rapidly under laissez-faire conditions, then you have no thorough knowledge either of

---

[12] Stamper, G., "Gustav Schmoller," in *Nord und Süd*, vol. 97, 1901, p. 309.

[13] In the authoritative Widener Library Shelflist, dealing with *Economics and Economic Periodicals*, vol. I, Cambridge, Mass., Harvard University Press, 1970, p. 815 lists this work as Zur Geschichte der deutschen *Klungenwerk* im 19. Jahrhundert.

history or political economy and you have no solid ground to stand on' (p. 42). In short, Schmoller meant to explode the cliches of the British and French political economists. "Go to the archives," he would say, "Get your feet wet and hands dirty. Collect all the statistics you can about the economic and social phenomena of a particular period. Describe all the material you find and only then begin to generalize. Be patient," he would add.

In addition to data on Prussia, the 1870 monograph presents comparable data for the states of Baden, Württemberg, Bavaria, and Saxony. Schmoller noted considerable over-staffing in a number of crafts in numerous tables. For instance, between 1801 and 1831, the number of master-craftsmen in relation to the population in Northern Germany remained constant. Yet at the same time, the country was undergoing rapid industrialization and many craftsmen found the rising competition hard to take.[14] Thereafter, Schmoller dealt with the transportation revolution in the early nineteenth century, in terms of canals and railroads and the rapid urbanization of Germany (p. 180). For instance, in 1856 Prussia's urban population was already 28.5% of the total population. The spreading Industrial Revolution affected profoundly the existing cottage industries and crafts, Schmoller noted, bestowing "unequal benefits to different social classes" (p. 661). He was greatly concerned, not to say upset, about the fast-growing inequality of income and property distribution (p. 662). He felt that the social consequences of rapid industrialization had thrown Germany into near chaos and into "a class-struggle situation" (p. 663). Schmoller felt that the doctrinaire demand for "economic freedom" was a cliche because there could be no competition between a lord and a landless peasant, or between a factory owner and a property-less factory worker (p. 682). Schmoller demanded social legislation to alleviate the misery and suffering of the factory workers (p. 693). He felt that the Prussian government had the obligation to protect the well-being of the lower classes and at the same time "tame the short-sighted egotistical urges" of the propertied classes. He did not believe that history worked itself out as a natural process; but rather that man must help by proper legislation. Already at that time Schmoller was intuitively afraid of the possible consequences of the spreading Marxist agitation among the working masses. Untrammeled laissez-faire was a social fiasco for him, and he was thinking very much along the lines that John Stuart Mill outlined in his chapter on the function of government in his *Principles of Political Economy.* Schmoller sincerely believed that the idea of justice should be used to build a better society, and that distributive justice was the key to his future legislative effort.[15] Alas, his 1870 monograph is available only in German, and Schmoller's monographs are now generally overlooked. To a mathematically trained economist today, Schmoller is a know-nothing historian!

---

[14] For a concise summary of this book in German, see Stamper, G., "Gustav Schmoller," in *Nord und Süd*, vol. 97, 1901, pp. 310-311.

[15] G. Schmoller, "The Idea of Justice in Political Economy," in *Annals of the American Academy*, vol. 4, 1893/94, pp. 697-737.

The second monograph from his years at Halle that deserves mention is Schmoller's work on the economic and social history of Prussia, which, by the way, was never quite finished. An English fragment of his *Studien über die wirtschaftliche Politik Friedrich des Grossen* was published as *The Mercantile System and Its Historical Significance: Illustrated Chiefly from Prussian History* in 1896. The well-known economic historian William J. Ashley did the translation. In this volume, which uses Prussia as a case study, Schmoller asserted that every phase of economic development was guided and controlled by a political organ (p. 2). He firmly rejected the idea that economic life was a process mainly dependent on individual action (p. 3-4). On the contrary, he argued that politics had always ruled the economic life of the mass of the people. With the rise of the territorial state from the 15th to 18th centuries, new territories and their institutions became the engines of social and economic change. Schmoller detailed how from the princely regalia emanated ordinances for the supervision of forests, hunting, fishing, mining, the use of streams, construction of dikes, regulation of schools, poor-relief, trade and industry, weights, and measures (p. 19). The territorial state strove for self-sufficiency (p. 25). Prussia, for example, considered its resources as a "whole, which ought, first of all, to serve the needs of the country; they ought not to enrich a few individuals, but serve the home producer and the home consumer at a fair price" (p. 31).

In the case of Prussia, Schmoller argued, "the state organization assisted the national economy" (p. 48). More specifically, the Prussian government gave unity to its "social life" (p. 49), and it was the Prussian government which brought about "a union for external defense and for internal justice and administration ..." (p. 49). Prussian mercantilism, like its counterparts, "in its innermost kernel ... is nothing but state making ... state making and national-economy making at the same time ..." (p. 50). For instance, "the great laws of Colbert in France of 1667, 1669, 1670, and 1673 founded the legal as well as economic unity of France" (p. 55). Prussia did the same.

The British in that mercantilist period pursued "a policy exclusively English" (p. 58). In the 1870s, when Schmoller wrote this monograph, the laissez-faire doctrine ruled supreme in British academic halls, and the "free traders" were extremely suspicious of the unpredictable and imperious bureaucracy. Schmoller raised this question:

Does it not sound to us today like the irony of fate, that the same England, which in 1750-1800 reached the summit of its commercial supremacy by means of its tariffs and naval wars, frequently with extraordinary violence, and always with the most tenacious national selfishness, ... at the very same time announced to the world the doctrine that only the egoism of the individual is justified, and never that of states and nations; the doctrine which dreamt of a stateless competition of all the individuals of every land, and of the harmony of the economic interests of all nations? (p. 80)

Schmoller was indeed suspicious of British economic doctrines. He despised their "harmony of interests" concept, and he was very critical of the "value of abstract generalization in economics."[16] He disliked theoretical speculations that lacked adequate observation, very much like Professor Wassily Leontief of New York University, who won the Nobel Prize in 1973 for his Input-Output analysis.

The triumph of laissez-faire, with its almost complete separation of the economy from government, continued virtually unabated during the first half of the nineteenth century.[17] That, of course, is a sweeping generalization. A few vigorous voices throughout Europe did dissent. Despite John Stuart Mill's objections against the untrammelled rule of laissez-faire, it prevailed through most of the 19th century, even in Germany, thanks to economists such as Christian J. Kraus of the University of Königsberg (today Kaliningrad of the Soviet Union), Georg Sartorius (1766-1828) of the University of Göttingen and particularly Karl H. Rau (1792-1870) and Hans von Mangoldt (1824-1868) and many others who preached the doctrine of laissez-faire in the academic halls of wisdom.[18] The naturalized Englishman, John Prince-Smith (1809-1875), residing in Germany, was particularly forceful in spreading the gospel of Adam Smith. The official spokesman of German liberal economists was the *Kongress deutscher Volkswirte*, established in 1858, which influenced German economic liberalism up to 1870.[19] Classical theories also had an iron grip on most academic economists in England, France, and to some extent even in Germany. They can be summed up as follows: (1) the law of self-interest and division of labor; (2) the law of diminishing returns; (3) the Malthusian law of population growth; (4) the iron law of wages; (5) the law of rent; (6) the law of capital accumulation; (7) the law of comparative advantage; (8) the law of value; (9) the quantity theory of money; and (10) Say's law of markets. These tenets were regarded as irrevocable and universally applicable regardless of time, place, or existing institutions. They were believed to operate in the same impersonal way as all physical laws and were held to be neither good nor bad, moral nor immoral, just immutable.[20] Yet Schmoller felt that government authorities had a duty to interfere in the market place to protect small businesses and economically weak segments of the population from strong, greedy, unscrupulous, or vicious representatives of the business community.[21] He was not the first who

---

[16] H. W. Spiegel (ed.), *The Development of Economic Thought. Great Economists in Perspective*, New York, John Wiley and Sons, 1952, p. 363.

[17] Winkel, H., "Der Umschwung der wirtschaftswissenschaftlichen Auffassungen um die Mitte des 19. Jahrhunderts," in *Wissenschaft und Kodifikation des Privatrechts im 19. Jahrhundert*, edited by Coing, H. and Wilhelm, W., Frankfurt M., Vittorio Klostermann, 1979, p. 3.

[18] *Ibid.*, pp. 3-4.

[19] *Ibid.*, p. 4.

[20] Rima, I. H., *Development of Economic Analysis*, Fourth Edition, Homewood, Illinois, Irwin, 1986, p. 167.

reacted vigorously against the doctrines of laissez-faire, and he turned away from it completely.[22]

Although the Classical School of Economics was firmly in the driver's seat in England up to roughly 1850, its much-acclaimed "invisible hand" and "social harmony" components soon became suspect. For instance, Thomas Carlyle (1795-1881) was one of the first to expose the prevailing social injustice to the industrial workers of England. In his 1839 book, *Chartism*, he described the bitter discontent among the working classes.[23] He said British workers were in effect demanding that Parliament and the ruling aristocracy "govern us properly. Otherwise, sheer necessity and law of nature will sweep you away." This was a powerful indictment of the laissez-faire state.[24] Another English economist, Walter Bagehot (1826-1877), the founder of the London *Economist* and the well-known author of *Lombardstreet* (1873), delivered a scathing attack on the prevailing business economics in 1879 in his book, *Economic Studies*. In it, he wrote that "the only ... safe ground of hope for Political Economy is, following Bacon's exhortation, to recommence afresh the whole work of economic inquiry."[25] A year earlier, in 1878, John K. Ingram, had attracted the attention of economists when he delivered an address on *The Present Position and Prospects of Political Economy* at the annual meeting of the Economic Sciences and Statistics Section of the British Association for the Advancement of Science.[26] He noted that the existing science of English political economy was "at a low ebb in public esteem."[27] Ingram felt that "one cause of error was to be found in its too abstract a deductive character,"[28] and he urged use of the inductive method by future economists. Finally, he pleaded that "the study of wealth cannot be isolated ... from other social phenomena."[29]

Another powerful critic of the deductive method of classical economics was Thomas Edward Cliffe Leslie (1827-1882). In his major work, *Essays on Political and Moral Philosophy* (1879), he attacked "the vicious abstraction" of English classical economists, which had done so much to darken economic inquiry.[30]

---

[21] Schmoller, G., *Zur Geschichte der deutschen Kleingewerbe im 19. Jahrhundert. Statistische und nationalökonomische Untersuchungen*, Halle, Verlag Waisenhaus, 1870, pp. 41-45.

[22] Winkel, H., *op. cit.*, p. 18.

[23] Symons, J., Editor, *Carlyle. Selected Works, Reminiscences and Letters*, London, Rupert Hart Davis, 1955, p. 260.

[24] *Ibid.*, p. 292.

[25] Bagehot, W., *Economics Studies*, London, Longman, 1911, p. 15.

[26] Ely, R. T., "Introduction," for Ingram, J. K., *A History of Political Economy*, London, A. C. Black Ltd., 1923, pp. vii-viii.

[27] *Ibid.*, p. viii.

[28] *Ibid.*, p. ix.

[29] *Ibid.*, p. xvii.

[30] Fetter, F. W., "Leslie T. E. Cliffe", in *International Encyclopedia of the Social Sciences*, vol. 9, New York, The Macmillan Company and The Free Press, 1968, p. 261.

Leslie criticized the cardinal doctrines of deductive economics as being attractive in their simplicity and symmetry but remote from actual fact.[31] Leslie's views were not popular among British economists, but he was a careful observer and well-traveled scholar, and he knew that the basic tenets of classical economics very often did not square with the facts in England, Ireland, and on the Continent. Frank Fetter once noted that Leslie's work had some influence in softening the rigidity of deductive economics, and his stimulating criticism of the purely deductive approach to economics had timeless relevance.[32]

Still another powerful critic of the classical economic doctrine and its unintended social consequences was Arnold Toynbee (1852-1883). His *Lectures on the Industrial Revolution of the Eighteenth Century* (1884, posthumous) contains his observations on the growth of English pauperism, the class hatreds, the Malthusian population doctrine, and the fictional "wage-fund" theory. One English historian wrote that it was a common view that, bad as was American slavery at that time, "white slavery in the manufactories of England was far worse."[33] Toynbee wanted to develop a new social policy as "a comprehensive alternative to socialism that would also be acceptable to the rest of society."[34] His aim was quite similar to that of Gustav Schmoller, for he advocated welfare policy via enlightened legislation. Like Schmoller, Toynbee believed that the historical approach was the most appropriate methodology for the analysis of contemporary social problems.[35] There were other important English economists of similar persuasion, like W. Cunningham and William J. Ashley (1860-1927), but these powerful English dissenters were really never incorporated into the body of mainstream economics.[36] Not even today. The young Schmoller was surely aware of the British dissenters.[37] He knew well that the doctrine of 'natural harmony' did not lead to 'social harmony.' He had read *Die Lage der arbeitenden Klasse in England*, the shattering report of the conditions of factory workers in England that found eager acceptance in Germany.[38] In 1844, Germany itself had

---

[31] Leslie, Thomas Edward Cliffe (1827-1882) in *Dictionary of National Biography*, vol. 11, p. 987.

[32] Fetter, F. W., *op. cit.*, p. 261.

[33] Lipson, E., *The Growth of English Society*, New York, Henry Holt and Company, 1950, p. 243.

[34] Kadish, A., *Apostle Arnold. The Life and Death of Arnold Toynbee, 1852-1883*, Durham, N.C., Duke University Press, 1986, p. 115.

[35] *Ibid.*, p. 124.

[36] Koot, G. M., *English Historical Economics, 1870-1920. The Rise of Economic History, and Neo-Mercantilism*, New York, Cambridge University Press, 1987.

[37] Ashley, W. J., "The Present Position of Political Economy in England," in *Die Entwicklung der deutschen Volkswirtschaftslehre im neunzehnten Jahrhundert. Gustav Schmoller zur siebzigsten Wiederkehr seines Geburtstages*, 24. Juni 1908, vol. I, Leipzig, Verlag von Duncker & Humblot, 1908, p. 9 and pp. 16-17.

[38] Friedenthal, R., *Karl Marx. Sein Leben und seine Zeit*, Munich, R. Piper and Company, 1981, p. 250.

been shocked to the core by the massive Weber-Revolte (Weaver's Revolt) of 1844 in Silesia.[39] And in 1848, the *Communist Manifesto* was another powerful indictment of the social conditions of the factory workers.

The social evils accompanying unchecked industrialization in England demonstrated that the "accumulation of wealth in the hands of merchants or manufacturers was inadequate by itself to fulfill the requirements of national well-being."[40] The appalling social misery of the working masses under laissez-faire led to the realization that the 'do-nothing government' or the 'night-watchman' government was inadequate to create social harmony. Marxists preached open class warfare and minced no words about their desire to overthrow the existing social order and replace it with the 'dictatorship of the proletarians.' Yet the doctrine of laissez-faire had gained considerable currency in the German industrial community, some government circles, and even some universities. However, a few German economists, known as German historical economists or economic historians, such as Wilhelm Roscher, Bruno Hildebrand and Karl Knies, not only rejected the claim of universal validity and applicability of classical economics, but insisted that it was grossly inadequate to deal with industrialization and its social consequences, not to speak of its irrelevance, for Germany.[41]

Before the emergence of the German Historical School of Economics, it was Friedrich List who had assailed Adam Smith's dictum that private enterprise, self-interest, competition and division of labor were applicable to all men anywhere in the world. Nations were in different stages of development and for this reason required different policy measures. Laissez-faire may have suited Britain in the late 18th and early 19th century, but "let alone" economic policies were useless for Germany and America. To catch up with Britain, List called for positive encouragement by government authorities. An industry, he said, must be protected before it could be established. Adam Smith's principles of political economy, therefore, were not of universal applicability, but were relative to time and place.

List's major work was the *National System of Political Economy*, published in 1841. As the title indicated, *the nation*, not the private profit-seeking business-man, was his main focus. The creation of value, by increasing specialization and expanding the scope for the division of labor, was of less importance to List than the capacity to produce values. The *power* of producing wealth was, for List, much more important than wealth itself. List was probably the first economist in the first third of the nineteenth century to abandon the laissez-faire ideas of British classical economists. He was a man of practical bent, for he knew civil

---

[39] Kroneberg, L. and Schloesser, R., *Weber-Revolte 1844*, Köln, Informationspresse and C. W. Leske Verlag, 1979, 617 pp.

[40] Lipson, E., *The Growth of English Society*, New York, H. Holt, 1950, p. 271.

[41] Winkel, H., *op. cit.*, p. 9.

service. He was a businessman at various times in his life. He was a prolific writer and a statesman as well. He decried let-alone individualism and the virtually "do-nothing" government of Adam Smith. He consistently pleaded for government intervention for the sake of national well-being and industrial advance.[42] List's message did not escape the German economists of the 1840's and 1850's in Germany.[43]

Wilhelm Roscher (1817-1894) is usually considered the first German economist who used 'the historical method' in his writings and who supposedly influenced Schmoller to become an academic.[44] In his 1843 work, known as *Grundriss*, for short, in his 1854 volume, *System der Volkswirtschaft*, and in his *Geschichte der Nationalökonomie in Deutschland* of 1874, Roscher emphasized that a single human being cannot be easily separated from society, language, religion, art, science, law, government, and the economy.[45] Roscher opposed what today is known as the "illegitimate isolation" of economic phenomena from the rest of society. He argued that law, government, and economics form a cluster of related fields of particular interest to economists, although he felt that economics was a sub-discipline of politics.[46]

Roscher's specific methodology consisted of four basic principles: 1) he combined economics with the history of law, government, and cultural evolution; 2) he cultivated economic history; 3) he used comparative methods of economic doctrines in different nations and different time periods; and 4) he used relativism to explain different economic policies over time.[47] A competent student of Roscher felt that his work was in many ways naive, and that it amounted to nothing but 'cultural morphology.'[48]

Throughout his writings, Roscher advocated an anti-revolutionary position[49] for the solution of pressing problems of the time. He differentiated sharply between reforms which resolve pressing problems in a peaceful manner on the basis of 'positive' law and those which advocate revolution, which, in Roscher's view, amounted to 'illegal acts', or in German, 'widerrechtliche Durchführungen.'[50] Revolutions for Roscher represented an 'immense misfor-

---

[42] Mitchel, B., *Great Economists in Their Times*, Totowa, N.J., 1966, p. 97.

[43] For the social, political, and economic background which led to the emergence of the German Historical School of Economics, see, Eisermann, G., *Die Grundlagen des Historismus in der deutschen Nationalökonomie*, Stuttgart, F. Enke Verlag, 1956, pp. 56-74.

[44] Eisermann, G., *ibid.*, p. 119.

[45] *Ibid.*, p. 139.

[46] *Ibid.*, p. 134.

[47] *Ibid.*, p. 152.

[48] *Ibid.*, p. 153.

[49] *Ibid.*, p. 143.

[50] Müssiggang, A., *Die soziale Frage in der historischen Schule der deutschen National-ökonomie*, Tübingen, J. C. B. Mohr (Paul Siebeck), 1968, p. 83.

tune.'[51] In the final analysis, Roscher believed economics should strive to discover 'laws of development' that show how nations progress from lower to higher economic, social, and moral stages of development.[52] His favorite tool was the use of analogy. Alas, Roscher failed to live up to his promise to create the kind of economics that would successfully cope with the shortcomings of the British classical economics and provide a respectable and workable answer to the Marxian challenge. It was Bruno Hildebrand (1812-1886) who stepped into the breach. By 1848, Hildebrand noted the corrosive hatred and deadly animosity of the classical school of economics.[53] He set out to save economics from 'false friends,' such as Friedrich List, Marxist socialists, and classical economics. In 1846, however, Hildebrand went to England and attended meetings with members of the German Communist Club. Upon returning to Germany, he was promptly relieved of his post as an elected president of the University of Marburg, as well as of his teaching position there.[54]

In 1848, Hildebrand published his *Die Nationalökonomie der Gegenwart und der Zukunft*, in which he pleaded for the 'reconciliation between capital and labor and suggested the necessary incorporation of the German working class as a responsible member of the reformed capitalistic economic and social order.'[55] What is more significant, Hildebrand wanted to keep economics from being a strictly academic discipline.[56] Almost one hundred and fifty years later, John Kenneth Galbraith would write in the United States that "departments of economics are graduating a generation of *idiots savants*, brilliant at esoteric mathematics yet innocent of actual economic life."[57]

According to Hildebrand, the primary duty of economists in their time was to fight the epigons of classical economics and socialists. Socialism to Hildebrand meant the grave of individuality and the end of human civilization.[58] He sounded like Aleksandr I. Solzhenitsyn today. In terms of normative economics, Hildebrand advocated sweeping social reforms for the purpose of making life more comfortable and tolerable to the masses of German industrial workers. Yet Hildebrand had no use for idle speculation and pleaded for the widest possible use of 'political and social measurements,' so as to provide the government with up-to-date information. His aim was to bridge the wide gap between the owners and non-owners of property via social legislation;[59] he had no use for socialism

---

[51] *Loc. cit.*

[52] Müssiggang, A., *ibid.*, p. 83.

[53] Eisermann, G., *op. cit.*, p. 159.

[54] *Ibid.*, p. 163.

[55] *Ibid.*, p. 164.

[56] *Ibid.*, p. 165.

[57] Colander, D. and Klamer, A., "The Making of an Economist," in *Economic Perspectives*, vol. 1, # 2, 1987, p. 95.

[58] Eisermann, G., *op. cit.*, p. 168.

[59] *Ibid.*, p. 174.

of any kind.[60] To prepare adequately for legislative reforms, Hildebrand advocated careful and detailed monographs on social and economic questions of the times. In this manner, Hildebrand had a profound influence on Schmoller a few decades later.[61]

Finally, Hildebrand felt that an economist must know life, and that he must have practical experience in order to grasp the real problems of his day. Classroom experience alone, in Hildebrand's view, was not enough, and laissez-faire, by itself, could not cope with the social consequences of rapid industrialization. Schmoller later called these social consequences a 'social fiasco' and also advocated legislative remedies. But Professor Eisermann in 1956 accused Hildebrand of having contributed to the 'theoretical bone softening' of German economics by placing less importance on economic theory than on the legislation needed to cope with the rising Marxist threat at that time.[62] Only those who have lived in the Stalinist Soviet Union know what Hildebrand and Schmoller felt in their bones, whereas Eiserman is still pushing theory for theory's sake!

In addition to Hildebrand, Karl Knies (1821-1898) provided further grist to the future mill of Gustav Schmoller, so to speak. In 1853, Knies published his *Die politische Ökonomie vom Standpunkte der geschichtlichen Methode*, which repeatedly emphasized that the classical prescription of natural harmony and laissez-faire did not lead to social welfare.[63] He was very much against the exclusive and absolute rule of the speculative economic theory of deductive type. He denied that such theory was valid for all people, at all times, and in all places.[64]

Knies also rejected the economist's method of 'illegitimate isolation' of economic phenomena from the rest of social factors. This much-practiced method of economists, for Knies, resembled 'ripped-out eyes, which see nothing;'[65] and constituted nothing more than 'intellectual aberration'. The classcial 'homo oeconomicus' was nothing but an 'abstract caricature' of reality and in many ways it was an inadmissible amputation.[66] Knies blamed the laissez-faire school of economics for the social decomposition of the newly industrialized Germany.[67] In fact, he felt that the negative social consequences of laissez-faire,

---

[60] *Ibid.*, p. 180.

[61] *Ibid.*, p. 184.

[62] *Ibid.*, p. 188.

[63] Eisermann, G., *ibid.*, p. 196.

[64] *Ibid.*, p. 202.

[65] Knies, K., *Die politische Ökonomie vom Standpunkt der geschichtlichen Methode*, 1853, p. 335. (Eisermann, p. 209).

[66] Eisermann, G., *op. cit.*, p. 209.

[67] *Ibid.*, p. 202.

or Schmoller's 'social fiasco,' actually amounted to a 'scientific justification of Marxist socialism.'[68]

But Knies disliked the much-advocated inevitability of a socialist future, and he hoped that the German historical school of economics would decisively defeat all socialist theories. He had no use for socialism. At the same time, he believed that his historically, institutionally, and statistically based economics would be able to cope successfully with the negative social aspects of laissez-fairism.[69] Knies considered statistics to be an independent science, which would prove invaluable in his valiant attempt to re-make economics.[70] Knies was the third big man of the early German Historical School of Economics. Like Roscher and Hildebrand, he strove to make economic inquiry more statistical, institutional, and historical. These three and other members of the early German Historical School of Economics had two specific objectives: 1) to fight and destroy the spreading socialist support for the overthrow of the existing social order, and 2) to overcome the legacy of the classical school of economics with its advocacy of 'natural harmony,' 'hands-off' government, and Manchester free trade policy.[71] This new breed of German economists wanted their discipline to become part of a broadbased social science, which paid attention to the unique features of the German economy. Finally, this new version of German historical economics should also become an ethically-based, teleological, and normative economics as well.

Schmoller was not the only economist who saw the growing discrepancy between formal equality and actual dependency under the auspices of laissez-faire. He saw with horror and consternation the unintended consequences of rapid industrialization of his native Germany. He also feared the spreading revolutionary fervor, particularly after 1848. The much discussed 'social question' boiled down to how to bridge the gap between the few rich factory owners and merchants and the propertyless industrial masses.[72] Already by the mid-1860's, Schmoller was asking how to integrate the new industrial masses into the mainstream of Germany society. He feared and dreaded the Marxist message and mission in his bones. He also knew what Roscher, Hildebrand, and Knies had to say about socialism. With this in mind, he raised the question of how to implement the demands raised by his three intellectual peers.[73]

---

[68] *Ibid.*, p. 202.

[69] *Ibid.*, p. 205.

[70] *Ibid.*, p. 193.

[71] Müssiggang, A., *op. cit.*, p. 209.

[72] Teuteberg, Hans-Jürgen, "Die Doktrin des ökonomischen Liberalismus und ihre Gegner dargestellt an der prinzipiellen Erörterung des Arbeitsvertrages im 'Verein für Socialpolitik' 1872-1905," in *Wissenschaft und Kodifikation des Privatrechts im 19. Jahrhundert*, edited by Coing, H. and Wilhelm, W., Frankfurt M., Vittorio Klostermann, 1977, p. 52.

[73] Winkel, H., "Der Umschwung der wirtschaftswissenschaftlichen Auffassungen um die Mitte des 19. Jahrhunderts," in *Wissenschaft und Kodifikation des Privatrechts im*

Schmoller knew that the laissez-faire system, by itself, would not solve the pressing social problems of the day.[74] He was not alone in expressing such sentiments. Lujo Brentano also cautioned German businessmen, journalists, and academics that laissez-faire was not a cure-all for the social ills of rapid industrialization and that welfare legislation might be in order soon. Schmoller also knew that German academic economists at that time, very much like today, were not interested in policy matters. The powerful, the mighty, and the tune-calling members of German society sneered at Schmoller and at like-minded economists who dared to doubt that universal benevolence, social harmony, and material bliss would result from the laissez-faire doctrine. Heinrich Bernhard Oppenheim,[75] one of the most influential journalists of the time, wrote a biting critique in the *Nationalzeitung* against Schmoller's book of 1870 and called Schmoller a *Kathedersozialist*, a lectern-socialist in English. Oppenheim said people like Schmoller amounted to nothing more than academic fools or bleeding hearts who should not be taken seriously. For Oppenheim and like-minded people of laissez-faire persuasion, economic liberalism with its immutable natural law concepts and 'hands-off' government policies, was near perfect.[76]

Schmoller was outraged at being dismissed as a *Kathedersozialist*. So was his friend Brentano, then a young academic economist teaching at the University of Berlin, who virtually itched to pick a fight with the influential Oppenheim. In order to do something concrete about the social misery of industrial workers in Germany, to counter the growing Marxist threat with its open class-war advocacy, and to clarify the social and labor questions of the day and propose legislative reform measures, Schmoller and some like-minded academics from a number of German universities formed a new organization. On July 13, 1872, a number of leading German academic economists of the day — Adolph Wagner, Wilhelm Roscher, Johannes Conrad, Ernst Engel, Georg Fr. Knapp, Lujo Brentano, and Julius von Eckardt — met in Schmoller's house in Halle to set up the *Kongress für soziale Reform*.[77] Professor Bruno Hildebrand was elected chairman, but discussions were conducted by Gustav Schmoller.[78] The new group decided to meet regularly to discuss the pressing social and economic problems of the day and to propose draft legislation for their amelioration.[79]

---

19. Jahrhundert, edited by Coing, H. and Wilhelm, W., Frankfurt M., Vittorio Klostermann, 1979, p. 9.

[74] Hintze, O., "Schmoller, Gustav v.," in *Deutsches Biographisches Jahrbuch. Überleitungsband II: 1917-1920*, Jena, 1928, p. 127.

[75] *Loc. cit.*; see also, Winkel, H., op. cit., p. 11.

[76] Albrecht, G., "Verein für Socialpolitik," in *Handwörterbuch der Sozialwissenschaften*, vol. 11, Stuttgart, G. Fischer, 1961, p. 10.

[77] Albrecht, G., "Verein für Socialpolitik," in *Handwörterbuch der Sozialwissenschaften*, vol. 11, Stuttgart, Gustav Fischer, 1961, p. 12.

[78] Boese, Franz, *Geschichte des Vereins für Sozialpolitik 1872-1932*, Berlin, Duncker and Humblot, 1939, p. 3.

People from many different professions and of similar reform-minded persuasion were invited to attend.[80] Schmoller and his friends ardently believed that only comprehensive reform for the working masses could preserve and improve the existing social order of Germany on the basis of private ownership of the means of production, market economy, and democratic parliamentary system of government. Schmoller had no use whatsoever for the Marxian class warfare and revolutionary panaceas. To him, Marxian socialism was nothing but "centralistic despotism," as he later wrote in his *Grundriss*.[81] So together with Lujo Brentano and many others, Schmoller launched a program for "a far-reaching program of social reform."[82] The first meeting of the new organization, which took place in Eisenach, in Thüringen (in today's German Democratic Republic) on October 6-7, 1872, marked the birth of the first economic policy-oriented association in the world.[83] At its inception, the new organization was guided by purely practical nature. Its aim was not to discuss economic principles but to air pressing social and economic problems, commission thorough studies, make surveys, and then make legislative proposals for remedying the situation.[84] In retrospect more than one hundred years later, Schmoller and his friends were taking the first modern steps towards the welfare state. But for Marxists, willfully blind and deaf, — then as now —, Schmoller's 'social reform' represented nothing but 'opportunistic deviation.' Only overthrow of the existing social order would do.

Some 158 people took part in the opening ceremonies of the Verein, according to Brentano,[85] whereas the History of the Verein für Socialpolitik listed 160 participants.[86] Schmoller gave the opening speech. With pathos he demanded that government and society at large take all the necessary steps to allow the swelling ranks of industrial workers to share in the material and spiritual prosperity of Germany.[87] Rudolf von Gneist was elected President of the new organization, and Lujo Brentano gave the first talk on prevailing factory legislation in Germany. His talk produced a storm of protest among industria-

---

[79] Wittrock, G., *Die Kathedersozialisten bis zur Eisenacher Versammlung 1872*, Berlin, 1939, dissertation, p. 3.

[80] Eckardt, J. v., *Lebenserinnerungen*, vol. I, Leipzig, Verlag von S. Hirzel, 1910, p. 275.

[81] Vol. I, p. 392.

[82] Asher, A., "Professors as Propagandists: The Politics of the Kathedersozialisten," in *Journal of Central European Affairs*, vol. 23, # 3, 1963, p. 282.

[83] Arndt, H., "Die wirtschaftliche Macht. Überlegungen anlässlich der 100-jährigen Wiederkehr der Eisenacher Tagung," in *Wirtschaftsdienst*, vol. 52, # 8, 1972, p. 1.

[84] Oberschall, A., *Empirical Social Research in Germany, 1848-1914*, The Hague, Mouton and Co., 1965, pp. 21-27.

[85] Brentano, L., *Mein Leben im Kampf um die soziale Entwicklung Deutschlands*, Jena, Eugen Diederichs Verlag, 1925, p. 78.

[86] Boese, F., *Geschichte des Vereins für Socialpolitik, 1872-1932*, Berlin, Duncker and Humblot, 1939, pp. 243-247.

[87] Boese, F., *ibid.*, pp. 6-11. See also Brentano, L., *op. cit.*, p. 79.

lists and among the daily press, which suggested that Brentano was guilty of inciting subversion.[88] Schmoller, the second speaker, dealt with labor unions and work stoppages. According to Lujo Brentano, he gave a superb speech, but it generated even more negative reaction than did Brentano's preceding address. Schmoller demanded sweeping factory legislation for which the German government was not quite ready. The daily press took Schmoller to task; some felt he, too, was engaged in social agitation.[89] But Brentano believed that the first meeting of the Verein had produced a permanent legacy: it had generated a socio-political interest among the 'have' classes, and had made the social welfare of the broad masses an abiding concern.[90]

Schmoller's sympathy for the fate of the rising industrial proletariat had begun long before 1872. In 1864 and 1865, he wrote three essays (*Die Arbeiterfrage*[91]) which deplored the almost unethical striving for wealth by the property-owning classes ["unsittlich hastiges Streben nach Besitz und Reichtum"] and the existence of two human classes, poor and rich, with nothing in the middle.[92] He said the unequal distribution of income was evil and that a healthy society needed a broad property-owning class.[93] He resented the exploitation of the poor and economically weak by the economically strong, upper classes. Yet he did not call for a socialist revolution to ameliorate the social misery of the industrial proletariat.[94] Instead, he advocated legislation to limit the working hours of children, teenagers, and women.[95] Schmoller's concern for the well-being of the German working classes inspired the work of the *Verein für Socialpolitik*, in English known as the Union for Social Politics, for years to come. For all Marxists, of course, Schmoller was not an *authentic socialist*,[96] because he was merely concerned with the advocacy of "building and sanitary codes, the legal limitation of the workday, protectionist legislation for women and children in industry, and the state management of railroads and post offices."[97]

Obviously, Schmoller was not afraid of spelling out his normative *ought to be's* and in the 1880's his advocacy inspired Germany to become the first industrial country in the world to enact welfare legislation. From the perspective of the

---

[88] Brentano, L., *ibid.*, p. 79.

[89] Brentano, L., *ibid.*, p. 80.

[90] Brentano, L., *ibid.*, p. 81.

[91] Originally published in *Preussische Jahrbücher*, vol. 14, in 1864 and vol. 15 in 1865.

[92] Albrecht, G., "Der junge Schmoller und die Arbeiterfrage," in *Schmollers Jahrbuch*, vol. 79, 1959, p. 517 and p. 518.

[93] *Ibid.*, p. 519.

[94] *Ibid.*, p. 525.

[95] *Ibid.*, p. 526.

[96] Schwendinger, H. and Schwendinger, R. R., *The Sociologists of the Chair*, New York, Basic Books, 1974, p. 95.

[97] *Ibid.*, pp. 86-87.

1980's, Schmoller clearly can be seen as one of the early fathers of the modern welfare state. He was not a mere 'academic propagandist' as Abraham Ascher described him in 1963.[98] For him, social science should be tested by its usefulness. Economics was not for the classroom exclusively, but an engine of analysis as Alfred Marshall put it a century ago.

Alas, academics forever strive for easy, eternal verities. With the launching of the *Verein* Schmoller's days in Halle were numbered.

---

[98] Ascher, A., "Professors as Propagandists: The Politics of the Kathedersozialisten," in *Journal of Central European Affairs*, vol. 23, 1963, pp. 292-302.

Chapter III

Schmoller in Strassburg, 1872-1882

Having conceived the idea of the *Verein für Socialpolitik* and having witnessed its splendid debut in 1872, Schmoller's tenure at the University of Halle was over. After seven years, he moved to the University of Strassburg where he remained for 10 happy years.[1] The old University was established in 1622.[2] After the Franco-Prussian War of 1870/71,[3] Alsace and Lorraine were re-annexed by Germany. It was a popular measure because both provinces were German-speaking and Alsace and Lorraine had been annexed by France earlier. Strassburg was an old German-speaking university where Goethe had once studied. Bismarck opposed the annexation, but had to give in to popular pressures. In 1872, Strassburg University became a German-speaking institution of higher learning, known as Kaiser-Wilhelm University.[4] Schmoller was brought to Strassburg by the *Kurator* of the University, Freiherr von Roggenbach.[5] According to Schmoller's colleague, Georg F. Knapp, Strassburg then looked like a provincial town of the seventeenth century, with miserable housing conditions and narrow, crooked streets. An ancient horse-shoe like building, called *Die Academie*, located in a rather run-down section of the town, was initially fixed up with a few lecture halls and classrooms. Yet the Reich government was generous and spent almost fourteen million marks on laboratories, equipment, and buildings.[6] Still the salient feature of the new university during the first decade of its existence was the young faculty; the majority was hardly older than thirty. There was a saying at that time that, at Strasssburg, the "assistant professors had been made full Professors."[7] This

---

[1] Schmoller, G., "Von der Strassburger Jubelfeier," in *Zwanzig Jahre deutscher Politik*, München and Leipzig, Duncker & Humblot, 1920, p. 203. See also, Fischer, W., "Schmoller, Gustav v.," in *International Encyclopedia of the Social Sciences*, vol. 14, New York, The Macmillan Company and The Free Press, 1968, p. 60.

[2] Paulsen, F., *The German Universities and University Study*, New York, Charles Scribner's Sons, 1906, p. 35.

[3] Stolper, G., Häuser, K., Borchardt, K., *The German Economy, 1870 to the Present*, New York, Harcourt, 1967, p. 19. See also, Gebhardt, *Handbuch der deutschen Geschichte*, vol. 33, Stuttgart, Union Verlag, 1960, pp. 184-187.

[4] Schmoller, G., "Die Bedeutung der Strassburger Universität," in *Zwanzig Jahre deutscher Politik*, München und Leipzig, Duncker & Humblot, 1920, p. 197.

[5] Knapp, G. F., *Einführung in einige Hauptgebiete der Nationalökonomie*, München and Leipzig, Verlag Duncker and Humblot, 1925, p. 365.

[6] Paulsen, F., *op. cit.*, p. 219.

[7] Schmoller, G., "Von der Strassburger Jubelfeier," in *op. cit.*, p. 205.

young faculty had a veritable thirst for factual knowledge and paid less attention to the utopian idealism of the bygone days, as was the case at the older, established German universities. The Strassburg faculty wanted to also take part in the practical affairs of the newly established German Reich. The universities and the Reich's administration, judiciary, and the parliament were to benefit from each other. Since the major purpose of this new German-speaking university was to bring German culture back to Alsace,[8] the Reich government financed it generously.[9] The new university had at first very few students, with even fewer students from the local region of Alsace and Lorraine. But a few curious youngsters from the Reich turned up and did not regret the experience, for in no time at all the University of Strassburg became an exemplary institution of higher learning.[10] By the third and fourth academic years, a few classes had already thirty or forty students. Within a very short time, Schmoller had become one of the most popular instructors at the university. He was not disturbed by small classes at first; in fact, he liked to hold his seminar with a very few selected students. His seminars were held once a week in his apartment, located at the Pariser Staden.[11] At that time, the seminar format was not widely practiced in Germany; soon, however, the University of Strassburg became known for its seminars.[12] Knapp characterized Schmoller as a great orator who held his powers almost to the end of his life. Schmoller supposedly needed a large audience to get going; then he could be eloquent, persuasive, and charming. In the classroom, he used to dictate some important sentences and thereafter comment on each. His students were said to be very attentive.[13] Sombart, on the other hand, once stated that Schmoller was ill at ease with large audiences and preferred small attentive audiences. Of course, large audiences in Strassburg were small audiences in Berlin. Schmoller was as fluent with the pen as he was with the spoken word. His very handwriting, according to Knapp, resembled women's handwriting in its clarity, and what he wrote was almost ready for the type-setter.[14] According to Stieda, Schmoller's tenure at Strassburg was marked by successful lecturing, creative research activity, and imaginative and innovative editorial ventures. In fact, his successful seminar was the reason why the University of Berlin eventually offered him a position.[15] He was also on very good terms with Friedrich Althoff, a Professor of French Law and an insider of

---

[8] Sheehan, J. J., *The Career of Lujo Brentano. A Study of Liberalism and Social Reform in Imperial Germany*, Chicago and London, The University of Chicago Press, 1966, p. 97.

[9] Schmoller, G., "Von der Strassburger Jubelfeier," in *op. cit.*, p. 205.

[10] Schmoller, G., "Die Bedeutung der Strassburger Universität," in *op. cit.,* p. 201.

[11] Stieda, W., "Zur Erinnerung an Gustav Schmoller und seine Strassburger Zeit," in *Schmollers Jahrbuch,* vol. 45, 1921, p. 227.

[12] Knapp, G. F., *op. cit.*, p. 365.

[13] Stieda, W., *op. cit.*, p. 227.

[14] Knapp, G. F., *op. cit.*, p. 366.

[15] n. a., *Reden und Ansprachen gehalten am 24. Juni 1908 bei der Feier von Gustav Schmollers 70. Geburtstag*, Altenburg,1908, p. 53.

3*

the university administration at Strassburg. Even though Alsace and Lorraine were annexed by the German Reich, the industrial relations of this region were still governed by a French law of 1864.[16] Hence, knowledge of it was of considerable importance. Subsequently, Friedrich Althoff became the future almighty bureaucrat in charge of the *Universitätsreferenz* section of the Prussian Ministry of Education, which confirmed all university appointments.[17] In any event, already in 1874-75 Schmoller was saying that economic activity cannot be, and should not be, forcefully or artifically separated from the total social activity; these were his first steps towards *Gesellschaftslehre*, i. e., a science about society or social life.[18] His colleagues in Strassburg included Wilhelm Lexis, the well-known statistician, and Georg F. Knapp, the author of the *Staatliche Theorie des Geldes*, who was also an excellent teacher.[19]

Within two years after his transplantation to Strassburg, Schmoller, at the age of 37, was elected by his colleagues, that is, full professors, to be the *Rector Magnificus* of the University for one year.[20] He was installed with much pomp and circumstance on October 31, 1874. His presidential address was *Strassburgs Blüte und die volkswirtschaftliche Revolution im XIII Jahrhundert.*[21] In this address, Schmoller dealt with the political and economic changes, the struggle between the city and the church, the change from barter to money economy, and the separation of the church's sphere of influence from that of the German Reich.

Schmoller's interest in the history of Strassburg started as soon as he arrived in Alsace. He embarked at once upon intensive research into the history of that city. Since he was interested in discovering the causes of changes of economic and social institutions over time—the Laws of Becoming—Schmoller and his students went to the local archives for information. Stieda, for instance, described how Schmoller had copied many original guild documents (*Zunftsurkunden*) und how these documents were read and discussed in his seminars. Participating students learned in this manner the entire evolution of the guilds and the related legalization of the various crafts as well. In discussing these documents, Schmoller eventually taught his students the significance of the inductive and the deductive methods in economic analysis.[22]

---

[16] Wehler, H. U., "Elsass-Lothringen von 1870 bis 1918: Das 'Reichsland' als politisch-staatsrechtliches Problem des zweiten deutschen Kaiserreiches," in *Zeitschrift für die Geschichte des Oberrheins*, vol. 109, 1961, pp. 133-199.

[17] Brocke, B. v., "Hochschul- und Wissenschaftspolitik in Preussen und im Deutschen Kaiserreich 1882-1907: das "System Althoff," in *Bildungspolitik in Preussen zur Zeit des Kaiserreichs*, Stuttgart, Klett-Cotta, 1980, p. 28.

[18] Stieda, W., *op. cit.*, p. 227.

[19] *Ibid.*, p. 231.

[20] Stieda, W., *op. cit.*, p. 259.

[21] Frensdorf, W., book review, in *Jahrbücher für Nationalökonomie und Statistik*, vol. 26, 1876, p. 221.

[22] Stieda, W., *op. cit.*, p. 228.

Another account also reported that Schmoller "opened local archives and placed his seminarists at work in them. He secured the cooperation of local officials and, in time, received grants of city money for the work of publishing the documents."[23] Joseph A. Schumpeter, in a different context, noticed that "though historical work done by economists was not in itself a novelty, it was then undertaken on an unprecedented scale and in a new spirit."[24] Schmoller's presidental address provided the first tentative results of his research in the long-term interlocking changes wrought by social, economic, and political factors. Mining the archives gave him a firmer grasp of the local chronicles and history and provided strong building blocks for the study of institutional change over time in wider and different settings.

Because Schmoller wanted to publish a monograph on the Cloth and the Weaver Guilds of Strassburg, he asked his younger colleague, Wilhelm Stieda, who hailed from Riga, to help him to collect material, do the preliminary drafts, and prepare the manuscript for the printer. Schmoller and Stieda were to be the authors of this intended monograph.[25] Stieda delivered the finished manuscript to Schmoller in December of 1877; on December 31, 1877, Schmoller replied that he had made substantive revisions of the manuscript.[26] Once Stieda saw the galleys of the manuscript, he asked Schmoller to drop his name from the title page. Schmoller at first refused, but eventually gave in to Stieda's stubbornness. It was done amicably, and in the preface of the book, Schmoller paid warm tribute to Stieda's contribution.[27]

The monograph, *Die Strassburger Tucher- und Weberzunft. Urkunden und Darstellungen nebst Regesten und Glossar. Ein Beitrag zur Geschichte der deutschen Weberei und des deutschen Gewerberechts von 13.-17. Jahrhundert*, according to Werner Sombart, another member of the Younger German Historical School of Economics, justified calling Schmoller a truly great economic historian.[28] Later on, in 1900, when Schmoller published the first volume of his *Grundriss*, some of this material, in the form of building blocks of long-term evolutionary change, was incorporated into the second and third chapter of Book Two, pp. 260-346, where Schmoller dealt with the structural transformation of societies over time and the role played by the cities in this process. The monograph on Strassburg, by the way, served later on as a

---

[23] Anderson, P. R., "Gustav von Schmoller (1838-1917)," in *Essay in Modern European Historiography*, edited and with an Introduction by S. William Halperin, Chicago and London, The University of Chicago Press, 1971, p. 298.

[24] Schumpeter, J. A., *History of Economic Analysis*, New York, Oxford University Press, 1954, p. 810.

[25] Stieda, W., *op. cit.*, p. 240.

[26] *Ibid.*, p. 243.

[27] *Ibid.*, pp. 244-245.

[28] Sombart, W., "Gustav Schmoller, 1838-1938," in *Der Deutsche Volkswirt*, July 1, 1938.

framework for Schmoller's rising interest in European economic development in general and of Prussia's economic and social transformation in particular. What emerged from this monograph was not so much the wealth of details on the various guilds, but the pattern of long-term evolution of economic and social institutions.[29]

During these years of teaching and writing, Schmoller was a much sought-after speaker. Nor did he shun a good public fight with his intellectual foes, be they left-leaning Marxists or right-wing reactionaries, or else the fanatical advocates of laissez-faire. Stieda, for instance, described Schmoller's public lecture of March 14, 1874, in Berlin, held in the Singakademie.[30] He dealt with the social question and the Prussian government.[31] Schmoller talked about the social consequences of the rapid industrialization of Germany and pleaded for the protection of the economically week segments of the population by promulgating necessary welfare legislation. He felt that industrialization had improved the status of the German working masses in political and legal but not in economic or social terms. Hence, the Prussian king, the bureaucracy, and the parliament ought to do something rapidly to raise the living conditions of the workers. Social justice demanded it, Schmoller felt. On that evening, with the Kaiser himself in the audience, Schmoller's lecture turned into a sensation, as Stieda called it.[32] At one point in his presentation Schmoller said that "one cannot make millions in contemporary Germany without touching with his sleeves the walls of a jail." Schmoller wanted to shake up the well-to-do classes and to remind them that they had an obligation to the working masses in terms of social welfare, social insurance, and adequate housing. Schmoller knew that the accumulation of wealth by manufacturers and merchants was by itself inadequate to fulfill the requirements of national well-being. And it was the young Schmoller who had already proclaimed that he wanted "no laissez-faire capitalism and no centralist despotism in the form of Marxist socialism."[33] In Stieda's view, Schmoller's physical appearance—his handsome face with a full black beard, his natural and easy-going bearing, lent impact to his delivery.[34] Schmoller's lecture led to a bitter controversy with the historian, Heinrich von Treitschke, over the role of the government in social and economic activities of the country. In the fall of 1875, Treitschke responded with *Der Sozialismus und seine Gönner. Nebst einem Sendschreiben an Gustav Schmoller*. Schmoller wrote a

---

[29] Stamper, G., "Gustav Schmoller," in *Nord und Süd*, vol. 97, 1901, p. 316.

[30] Stieda, W., *op. cit.*, pp.. 222-223.

[31] Francke, E., "Gustav Schmoller und die Sozialreform," in *Soziale Praxis und Archiv für Volkswohlfahrt*, vol. 24, # 44, 1917, p. 863.

[32] Stieda, W., *op. cit.*, p. 223.

[33] For a superbly argued modern work on this topic in German, see *Weder Kommunismus noch Kapitalismus*, edited by R. v. Bruch, München, Verlag, C. H. Beck, 1985, pp. 7-19.

[34] Stieda, W., *op. cit.*, p. 223.

spirited reply—*Über einige Grundfragen des Rechts und der Volkswirtschaft. Ein offenes Sendschreiben an Herrn Prof. Dr. Heinrich v. Treitschke*, also in 1875. At issue was the burning question: how to deal with the social consequences of the rapid industrialization of Germany? By the mid-1870's, Karl Marx had already published his first volume of *Das Kapital*; the working classes had already been mesmerized by his Communist Manifesto of 1848.[35] His message—"Proletarians, get rid of your exploiters, the bloodsuckers of the working class; take away their property and become the dominant class"—had an incredibly strong appeal. In the 1840's, the social nightmare of rapid industrialization in England and Germany was frightening, but since the Marxist rule had not yet been put into practice, the working masses and many intellectuals were looking forward to it with eager anticipation. Ferdinand Lasalle (1825-1864) was busy throughout Germany organizing the industrial workers into a Workers' Party.[36] He advocated the destruction of the laissez-faire type government and its replacement by a "strong" worker's government; he also pleaded for the eventual elimination of private property.

By the mid-1870's, Albert F. E. Schäffle had published his influential *Kapitalismus und Sozialismus*. To Schmoller it was one of Schäffle's best books.[37] Schäffle, like Schmoller, did not like the wide and crass class differences in the rapidly industrializing Germany. Within this milieu, Schmoller presented, in 1875, the basic demand of a more equitable distribution of national income. He emphatically rejected the prevailing social selfishness and the exploitation of the weak by the strong.[38] His idea of social justice was elevated to the guiding principle of a reform programm.[39] Schmoller was very much aware that it was high time to limit the privileges of the bourgeois class and to do something concrete for the industrial workers, living at bare subsistence level. What is curious about Schmoller at the time was that he was not a doctrinaire economist, but a young academic with a warm heart, a cool mind, and open eyes and ears. He was not a captive of some doctrine or technique; he wanted to preserve the existing social order of Germany, with private ownership of the means of production, with parliamentary democracy, and with the Kaiser at the head of the German nation. But he also wanted to bring about rapid improvement in the

---

[35] For a recent evaluation of the Manifesto, see Friedenthal, R., *Karl Marx. Sein Leben und seine Zeit*, München, R. Piper and Co., 1981, pp. 326-336.

[36] Gide, C. and Rist, C., *A History of Economic Doctrines*, New York, D.C. Heath and Co., 1913, p. 433-436. For a recent, somewhat impressionistic volume, on Lasalle, see, Bleuel, H. P., *Ferdinand Lasalle oder der Kampf wider die verdammte Bedürfnislosigkeit*, Frankfurt M., Fischer Taschenbuch Verlag, 1982, pp. 310-314.

[37] Schmoller, G., "Albert E. Fr. Schaeffle, (1879-1888)," in *Zur Litteraturgeschichte der Staats- und Sozialwissenschaften*, (Reprint), New York, Burt Franklin, 1968, p. 213.

[38] Albrecht, G., "Der junge Schmoller und die Arbeiterfrage," in *Schmollers Jahrbuch*, vol. 79, 1959, p. 8.

[39] Kromphardt, W., "Die Überwindung der Klassenkämpfe nach Gustav von Schmoller," in *Schmollers Jahrbuch*, vol. 62, 1938, pp. 333-348.

living standards of the toiling masses.[40] Schmoller's interest in the welfare of the working masses began in the 1860's, when he, together with Ferdinant Lasalle, deplored the social misery caused by the early and rapid industrialization of his native country under the auspices of laissez-faire. Schmoller warned that the lower classes also had a right to derive benefits from increased production. He feared that the industrial masses would not forever accept a social order which tolerated glaring discrepancies in its economic rewards.[41] In short, Schmoller was very much afraid of a Marxist-led revolution. For this reason, he was often dubbed "the bleeding heart lectern socialist", or "sugarwater socialist." In turn, Schmoller urged the Prussian government to push relentlessly for large-scale integration of the German industrial workers by means of an active, forward-looking *Sozialpolitik*, something that today is called "welfare legislation." Such Schmoller initiatives for decades were defamed and maligned by Marxist socialists as well as by German arch conservatives. For example, Karl Kautsky, the leading German Marxist at that time, attacked and sneered at Schmoller for decades. For example, he argued that Schmoller's welfare legislation is nothing but "an attempt to buy off the union leaders."[42] He claimed that industrialization had brought little visible material progress to the working masses and the exploitation had continued unabated.[43] Since privately owned means of production constituted the source of exploitation and oppression, Schmoller's peacemaking efforts, via social welfare legislation, between capital and labor was nothing but daydreaming, a reactionary utopia, an opportunistic distortion.[44] Kautsky, of course, could not imagine the hardships of the industrial workers in the Soviet Union a few decades later. In any event, Schmoller was attacked and vilified not only from the left, but from the arch conservative right as well. As already noted, the historian Heinrich von Treitschke, disliking Schmoller's program, also took him to task; although Treitschke himself was not an opponent of reforms, he feared that the proposed social legislation, a là Verein für Socialpolitik, would "turn the workers into parasites who were to work no more than four to six hours a day, spending the rest of their time sleeping, drinking, and talking."[45] Treitschke must have been willfully blind or captive to some dogma for not seeing all the social suffering and misery around him in the wake of the deep economic recession in the period between 1873 und 1875.[46] This

---

[40] Lütge, Fr., "Gustav von Schmoller als Sozialpolitiker," in *Schmollers Jahrbuch*, vol. 62, 1938, pp. 189-211.

[41] Dorpalen, A., *Heinrich von Treitschke*, New Haven, Yale University Press, 1957, p. 198.

[42] Kautsky, K., "Schmoller über den Fortschritt der Arbeiterklasse," *Die Neue Zeit*, vol. 22, # 2, 1904, p. 229.

[43] *Ibid.*, p. 231.

[44] *Ibid.*, p. 236.

[45] Dorpalen, A., *op. cit.*, p. 200.

[46] Stolper, G., *This Age of Fable*, New York, Reynall and Hitchcock, 1942, pp. 6-7. See also, Stolper's *German Economy, 1870-1940*.

was, in the words of knowledgeable authors, "a sad time" for all industrial countries of the world.[47] Schmoller argued that the central government had "a moral duty to alleviate undue hardships."[48] Treitschke, on the other hand, viewed Schmoller's proposed social reforms as a "threat to the stability of the young German state."[49] For Schmoller, the proposed legislation designed to provide protection against the economically strong–unemployment compensation, a hygienic housing policy, the right to form a labor union, and health and disability insurance for the industrial workers—was the only way to assure social peace and long-term economic growth of Germany.[50] A similar program was proposed by John Stuart Mill[51], who among other things, called for government involment in education and for protection of children and women from abuse and excessive hours of factory work, but it took the British Parliament decades to catch up with the social legislation of Germany.[52] After Schmoller's transplantation to Berlin, he continued to push for social welfare legislation. Schmoller insistently pleaded for greater social justice and for planned welfare legislation initiated by the socially-minded Prussian royal house and by the elite bureaucracy.[53] His essay, *The Idea of Justice in Political Economy*, is one of the very few items that were translated into English during his lifetime.[54] The idea of social justice was the *loadstar* of his actions in life and of his advocacy of social reform in the Verein, as stressed by Schmoller's successor at the University of Berlin, Heinrich Herkner.[55] Schmoller hoped that this welfare legislation would be realized with the able assistance of the Prussian king, a concept he called *soziales Königtum.*[56]

Busy as Schmoller was, in 1881, he was made editor of the *Jahrbuch für Gesetzgebung, Verwaltungs- und Gewerberecht*, which later became to be known as *Schmollers Jahrbuch*. Even though Schmoller constantly wrote, did research,

---

[47] Stolper, G., Häuser, K., and Borchardt, K., *The German Economy, 1870 to the Present*, New York, Harcourt, Brace and World, 1967, p. 20. See also, Treue, W., *Wirtschaftsgeschichte der Neuzeit*, Stuttgart, A. Kröner Verlag, 1962, pp. 543-547.

[48] Dorpalen, A., *op. cit.*, p. 200.

[49] *Ibid.*, p. 203.

[50] Herkner, H., "Gedächtnisrede auf Gustav von Schmoller," in *Schriften des Vereins für Socialpolitik*, vol. 159, 1919, p. 14.

[51] Mill, J. St., *Principles of Political Economy, with Some of Their Applications to Social Philosophy*, Revised Edition, vol. 2, New York, The Colonial Press, 1900, pp. 456-463.

[52] Ritter, G. A., *Social Welfare in Germany and Britain. Origins and Developments*, New York, Berg, 1986, 211 pp.

[53] Spiethoff, A., "Gustav Schmoller," in *Schmollers Jahrbuch*, vol. 42, 1918, p. 12.

[54] See *Annals of the American Academy of Political and Social Science*, vol. 4, 1893/94, pp. 697-737.

[55] Herkner, H., *op. cit.*, p. 12.

[56] Bruch, R. v., "Bürgerliche Sozialreform im deutschen Kaiserreich," in *Weder Kommunismus noch Kapitalismus. Bürgerliche Sozialreform in Deutschland vom Vormärz bis zur Ära Adenauer*, München, Verlag C. H. Beck, 1985, p. 68.

and edited the monograph series which he had launched, as well as his *Jahrbuch*, he took his teaching obligations and seminar duties seriously.[57] One of his students wrote that his classes were the *driving and creative force* of his research activity. At the lectern he was quite formal; whereas in the seminar Schmoller was at his very best. When in a good mood, he could laugh off everything, but when not in a sanguine mood, Schmoller could be biting. He often used to ask: "Does anyone have anything to add? If not, I shall proceed."[59] Finally, in his classes Schmoller strove to be as *anschaulich* (realistic) as he possibly could, so as to give the beginning student an idea of the concatenations of social phenomena. He never pretended that life and economics are simple. As a true Humboldtian scholar, Schmoller was both creator of *new* knowledge and an effective transmitter of *existing* knowledge.

In Strassburg, together with Wilhelm Lexis, Georg Knapp, and Wilhelm Stieda, he regularly held an economics seminar. The papers presented were edited and later published as monographs in a series known as *Staats- und sozialwissenschaftliche Forschungen*. After 1878 they were regularly published by Duncker and Humblot Verlag of Berlin.[60] The publications emphasized the meticulous collection of primary material, insisted on detailed description, and quantification if possible, with a minimum of speculation. Description in the process of learning, understanding, and evaluating social statistics was of utmost importance. Schmoller did not want to build his proposals for social reform on the quicksand of speculation. For this reason, his monographs and his statistical surveys were designed to obtain a thorough picture of the existing reality.[61] Schmoller felt that only on the basis of comprehensive and solid factual material would it be possible to provide a solid foundation for eventual legislative action.[62] Neither did Schmoller encourage quick generalization for academic economists. He aimed to amass enough information in decades to come to substantiate the eventual *laws of becoming*. Only then, would he venture to do synthesis.

---

[57] Spiethoff, A., "Gustav v. Schmoller," in *Schmollers Jahrbuch*, vol. 42, 1918, p. 16.

[58] Simon, H., "Schmoller als Lehrer," in *Die Zukunft*, vol. 86, 1914, pp. 122-23.

[59] *Ibid.*, p. 124.

[60] Hintze, G., Spiethoff, A., and Beckerath, E. v., *op. cit.*, p. 336.

[61] Müssiggang, A., *Die soziale Frage in der historischen Schule der deutschen National-ökonomie*, Tübingen, J. C. B. Mohr (Paul Siebeck), 1968, pp. 8-10.

[62] Bruch, R. v., *op. cit.*, p. 66.

Chapter IV

Working at Full Steam in Berlin

In 1882, after ten years of successful and busy academic life at the University of Strassburg, Schmoller moved to the University of Berlin. He had been nominated for an appointment in Berlin twice before, in 1870 and in 1879, but was rejected both times. The Prussian Ministry of Education supposedly did not consider him the right person because of his persistent advocacy of social and welfare reform for the working masses[1] and emancipation of the German proletariat.[2] Thus, in 1870, the position was offered to Wilhelm Roscher, who turned it down, and then to Adolph Wagner, who accepted it.[3] Only upon the accidental death of Professor Adolf Held were the objections against Schmoller dropped. In June 1880, he was finally offered the chair. At first, however, he was afraid his health would not allow him to accept.[4] In 1881, he had complained to Wilhelm Stieda that for almost three-quarters of that year he had been working with "double steam" (*doppeltem Dampf*), and had run out of energy.[5]

At the time he took Held's chair,[6] Schmoller had one reasonably close friend in the Economics Department — Adolph Wagner. But in many ways Schmoller was quite reserved about Wagner's ideas.[7] In methological matters particularly the two were far apart.

Schmoller had hardly settled into his new post when he got involved in the academic duel of his life, with the Viennese economist, Carl Menger (1840-1921), the founder of the Austrian School of Economics.

All social scientists have heard of this bitter, prolonged, and acrimonious controversy as the *Methodenstreit* of the 1880's. The term *Methodenstreit* refers to "Battle Over Appropriate Methods in Economics." As a rule, most of the

---

[1] Hintze, O., Spiethoff, A., and Beckerath, E. v., "Gustav von Schmoller, (1838-1917)," in *Lebensbilder grosser Nationalökonomen*, edited by Horst C. Recktenwald, Köln und Berlin, Kiepenheuer and Witsch, 1965, p. 33.

[2] Rivinius, K. J., "Einführung," in *Die soziale Bewegung in Deutschland des neunzehnten Jahrhunderts*, edited by Rivinius, K. J., München, Heinz Moos Verlag, 1978, p. 17.

[3] Wittrock, G., *Die Kathedersozialisten bis zur Eisenacher Versammlung 1872*, Berlin, Verlag Dr. Emil Ebeling, 1939, p. 81.

[4] Stieda, W., "Zur Erinnerung an Schmoller und seine Strassburger Zeit," in *Schmollers Jahrbuch*, vol. 45, 1921, p. 253.

5 *Ibid.*, p. 254.

[6] Epstein, M., "Obituary. Schmoller," in *Economic Journal*, vol. 27, 1917, p. 435.

[7] Wittrock, G., *op. cit.*, p. 81.

popular accounts of this controversy in English depict Schmoller as a flaming Prussian nationalist, economic historian and social reformer, and Menger as the cool, sophisticated co-founder of the marginal school of economics of Vienna. Menger emerged the winner and in the mainstream economics of today the defeat of the German Historical School of economics is known as the Revolution of the Marginal School of Economics.[8]

Actually, as Eisermann suggested in the mid-1950's, the real antipode of Menger was not Schmoller but Wilhelm Roscher[9] for whom Schmoller was a sort of stand-in. In 1883, Wilhelm Dilthey, the philosopher and colleague of Schmoller at the University of Berlin, published the first two books of his much acclaimed work under the title, *Introduction to the Social Sciences.*[10] By coincidence, also in 1883, Carl Menger published his *Inquiry into the Method of the Social Science.*[11] In this work, Menger sided with the pure theorists and their method of isolating of economic variables from the rest of social phenomena. He vigorously defended the necessity of the deductive method, and was not particularly complimentary in his treatment of the work of the two schools of the German Historical School of Economics.

Schmoller read the book and wrote a lengthy review article in 1883 which came to be known as *The Writings of C. Menger and W. Dilthey on the Methodology of Political and Social Sciences.*[12] Schmoller did not like what Menger wrote, and he questioned the merits, relevance and excessive reliance on deduction in the social sciences of his day, particularly in economics.[13] Schmoller used Dilthey's work to demonstrate that Menger's book beamed the light in the wrong direction and should not be taken seriously. He felt that Menger's reliance on deduction was appropriate in the natural sciences, but near-useless in the study of man and society. Schmoller strongly opposed easy and quick generalizations based on insufficient observation and unquestioning deference

---

[8] Kauder, E., *A History of Marginal Utility Theory*, Princeton, Princeton University Press, 1965; see also Stigler, G., "The Adoption of the Marginal Utility Theory," in *The Economics as Preacher and Other Essays*, Chicago, Illinois, The University of Chicago Press, 1982, pp. 72-85.

[9] Eisermann, G., *Die Grundlagen des Historismus in der deutschen Nationalökonomie*, Stuttgart, Ferdinand Enke Verlag, 1956, p. 119.

[10] *Einleitung in die Geisteswissenschaften. Versuch einer Grundlegung für das Studium der Gesellschaft und der Geschichte.* For an introduction into Dilthey's work in English, see Lane, F.C. and Riemersma, J.C., "Introduction to Arthur Spiethoff," in *Enterprise and Secular Change*, Homewood, Ill., Irwin, 1953, pp. 431-440.

[11] *Untersuchungen über die Methode der Socialwissenschaften und der politischen Oekonomie insbesondere.* The English version of this book is known as *Problems of Economics and Sociology*, Urbana, Illinois, University of Illinois Press, 1963, 237 p.

[12] Schmoller, G., *Zur Literaturgeschichte der Staats- und Sozialwissenschaften*, Leipzig, 1888; reprinted in New York, by Burt Franklin, 1968, pp. 275-304.

[13] For an interesting account of this matter, see Czaplicki, M., *Schmoller als Sozialökonom. Eine kritische Beleuchtung seiner theoretischen und sozialpolitischen Ansichten*, Breslau, F.W. Junger, 1929, pp. 39-46.

to the basic laws of economic science. He demanded instead meticulous description, patient study of the archival materials, collection of as much statistical material as possible, and proper introspection of the various interdependencies among the economics, social, political, institutional, and psychological factors. Schmoller never departed from these norms. As he wrote in the Preface to the second volume of his *Grundriss*: "I wanted to liberate economic theory from the wrong abstractions by means of exact historical, statistical and economic research."[14] Schmoller was not interested in economic theory per se; his concern was to collect the required material and to use it as a necessary input for social legislation, designed to raise the economic and social well-being of the German industrial masses.[15] His main aim in life was to prevent the emergence of "centralistic despotism" of Marxists by means of continuous social legislation. Schmoller was building the early foundations of the modern welfare state, whereas Carl Menger, the economic theorist, was at his best as a scientist and was less concerned with the pressing social problems of the day.

A year later, Menger fired his second salvo in the battle of wits by publishing *Die Irrthümer des Historismus in der deutschen Nationalökonomie.*[16] Menger and Schmoller locked horns and held firmly for a long time to their initial positions. The swarm of followers of the two spokesmen also locked horns, and the economics profession wasted two decades quarreling about methodology. Schumpeter once referred to those two decades as "nothing but a history of wasted energies."[17] A decade later the antagonists softened their early rigid positions on deduction and induction, lowered their voices, and in 1911 Schmoller wrote that for an economist both methods were indispensable.[18] Schmoller's 1911 article represented not a retreat from his earlier position but a careful modification of his initial rigid insistence on the primacy of induction. In that article, Schmoller spelled out how to cope with data collection problems and how to evaluate the material collected. He suggested five distinct steps:

1. observation and recording of observations;
2. description of observed material according to statistical methods by way of a sample or by way of monographs using historical method;
3. definition and classification of the material on hand;
4. attempt to isolate causes via causal analysis, and
5. formulation of regularities and possible empirical laws.

---

[14] *Grundriss II*, p. VI.

[15] Schäfer, U. G., *Historische Nationalökonomie und Sozialstatistik als Gesellschaftswissenschaften*, Köln, Böhlau Verlag, 1971, p. 93.

[16] Published in Vienna, by A. Holder, 87 pp.

[17] Schumpeter, J. A., *History of Economic Analysis*, New York, Oxford University Press, 1954, p. 814.

[18] Schmoller, G., "Volkswirtschaft, Volkswirtschaftslehre und -methode," in *Handwörterbuch der Staatswissenschaften*, vol. 8, Jena, Verlag von Gustav Fischer, 1911, p. 478.

These prescribed steps in the material collection suggest that Schmoller could be likened to a physician who does a physical examination to look for signs and symptoms of an illness. Schmoller was not concerned with classroom economics; instead he strove to create a "realistic science" of society.

In fact, Schmoller noted that people who talk politics and social issues would err less frequently if they were more familiar with the research methods of the physical sciences. Schmoller's experience had taught him that purely mathematical sciences and their techniques hindered the making of correct political and economic inferences, analysis, or assessments.[19] Eventually, the controversy petered out, as Charles Gide and Charles Rist, in their well-known textbook, noted that "induction and deduction are both necessary for the science, just as the right and left foot are needed for walking."[20] However, this controversy continued to fascinate economists.[21] Long after the eventual reconciliation of the two opposing camps, Schmoller continued to hesitate to present economic and social problems in a simplistic manner. For this reason, he always stressed the purely hypothetical element in all theoretical formulations, be it an hypothesis, an "as-if" statement, or a mathematical model, which Schmoller did not employ. Because Schmoller listened to the opposing opinion in discussing economic and social matters, he was dubbed a vague relativist. In addition, Schmoller stressed that time and place play an enormous role in the analysis and policy recommendations of economic and social issues. He rejected, out of hand, all simplistic, mono-causal explanations of micro- und macroeconomic phenomena.[22] This may have been the reason why Carl Menger, in his obituary on Schmoller, wrote that he lacked the necessary background for theoretical work.[23]

Berlin, in still other ways, opened another chapter of Schmoller's busy life. In addition to the various duties at the University, the Verein für Socialpolitik and the editorship of the *Schmollers Jahrbuch, Acta Borussica*, and the monograph series, Schmoller was appointed and elected to many posts and showered with honors. For instance, in 1884, he became a member of the Prussian Council of State and, in 1887, a member of the Prussian Academy of Sciences. In 1899, he

---

[19] Schmoller, G., *ibid.*, p. 481.

[20] Gide, C. and Rist, C., *A History of Economic Doctrines*, New York, D.C. Heath, 1913, p. 397. See also Spiethoff, A., "Gustav v. Schmoller," in *Schmollers Jahrbuch*, vol. 42, 1918, p. 24.

[21] Ritzel, G., *Schmoller versus Menger. Eine Analyse des Methodenstreits im Hinblick auf den Historismus in der Nationalökonomie*, Offenbach/Main, Bollwerk-Verlag, 1951, 148 pp. and Mises, L., "Soziologie und Geschichte. Epilog zum Methodenstreit in der Nationalökonomie," in *Archiv für Sozialwissenschaft und Sozialpolitik*, vol. 61, 1929, pp. 465-512. Also, still useful, is Kaufmann, F., *Methodology of the Social Sciences*, New York, Oxford University Press, 1944, pp. 212-228.

[22] Hintze, O., Spiethoff, A., Beckerath, E. v., *op. cit.*, p. 337, 2nd paragraph.

[23] Menger, C., "Schmoller," in *Almanach der Akademie der Wissenschaften*, Vienna, vol. 68, 1920, p. 450.

became a member of the Prussian Upper House as a representative of the University of Berlin.[24] In 1897, Schmoller was elected *Rector Magnificus* of the university, to be addressed as *Seine Magnifizenz*. His formal acceptance speech was given on October 15, 1897, and it was later published as *Wechselnde Theorien und feststehende Wahrheiten im Gebiete der Staats- und Socialwissenschaften und die heutige deutsche Volkswirtschaftslehre*.[25] Schmoller's long address touched upon all aspects of economics of the day. He admonished the audience that hard scientists, like physicists, always arrived at the same conclusion in explaining a particular phenomenon, whereas in social sciences this is not the case. To understand how society works and evolves, an economist must know something about its customs, laws, institutions, and social statistics. Such an understanding could be obtained only by practicing what Schmoller called a *Detailkenntnis*, i.e., a thorough knowledge of social and institutional detail (p. 9). He ridiculed the naive, childish optimism of the laissez-faire school of economics and the "scientific socialists," known as Marxists. He rejected the classical school of economics as well as Marxism as too speculative because both schools of thought had neglected to do the preliminary spadework of detailed investigations of the historical, social, and institutional phenomena (p. 12). The schools were actually the twin offsprings of the same speculative rationalism, the fading and crumbling pillars of the French Enlightenment of the eighteenth century. To replace the intellectual scaffoldings of Adam Smith and Karl Marx, Schmoller advocated the construction of a new social science, which encompassed the nation, its government, society, and economy (p. 19). In this effort, detailed monographic research would be indispensable. He also suggested that the roles of individuals and government in society should become a focus of economists' attention. He was particularly concerned with what he called the "harmonization" of the private and public sectors in society. Schmoller felt that the "laissez-faire" school of economics (1) was inadequate to cope with the pressing social problems of the 1890's; (2) could not provide solutions for dealing with the emerging new forms of business enterprise; (3) could not deal adequately with the unintended consequences of competition; (4) was unable to explain the ongoing bitter trade rivalry all over the world among the major industrial countries, and (5) proposed no solution to problems faced by economically and demographically small countries of the world (p. 22). Finally, Schmoller said that in economics all knowledge must be put to use, it must serve the society in coping with the pressing social problems of the day (p. 23). He was happy to note that his German Historical School of Economics had been active in making numerous social reform proposals (p. 25) and he was obviously thinking of his efforts in the *Verein für Socialpolitik*. In a way, Schmoller was thinking of economics as *praxeology*, a general theory of purposeful action, and thus anticipating the

---

[24] Epstein, M., "Obituary. Gustave Schmoller," in *Economic Journal*, vol. 27, 1917, p. 435.

[25] Berlin, Buxenstein, 1897, 32 pp.

seminal work of Eugen Slutsky (1926) in which the social system, time, activity, purpose and the concept of economic power were all intertwined.[26] Schmoller concluded by saying that, in his new school of economics, the human being and his welfare would be the focus of investigation, not capital formation or commodities, as it had been in the classical economics or Marxism. This last clue was of particular importance in understanding the structure of his *Grundriss*, which he was writing at that time.

Not everybody liked what Schmoller had to say. One interesting objection to Schmoller's speech was raised by Professor A. A. Issaieff of the University of St. Petersburg. He rejected Schmoller's assertion that the theoretical foundations of the classical economics of Smith, Ricardo, and Mill represented the dead hand of the past to be put away *ad acta*. On the contrary, argued Issaieff, the classical economics represented the "permanent legacy of our science."[27] It was also incorrect to assert that the Viennese Marginalist School of Economics had created nothing new.[28] In fact, according to Issaieff, Böhm-Bawerk's work was received in Russia as a revelation. And, finally, Adam Smith's system of natural harmony called only for a "nightwatchman" type government whereas John Stuart Mill called for government intervention in many areas of economic life, a plea which was quite similar to that of Schmoller. But Schmoller lumped all British economists into one batch of 'non-interventionists.'[29]

Busy as Schmoller was, he became known as the "Professormaker or unmaker."[30] This was probably an overstatement, but it was true that Schmoller was a close friend and adviser of Friedrich Althoff (1839-1908), who was appointed in 1882 to modernize the German educational and university systems at the Ministry of Education in Berlin. Althoff had been a colleague of Schmoller's at the University of Strassburg, where Althoff worked from 1871 to 1882 as a university administrator as well as Professor of French Law and modern Civil Law.[31] At the Ministry of Education, Althoff was in charge of the *Universitätsreferenz*, which decided on all university appointments.[32] He was facetiously called the "secret" Minister of Education or the "Bismarck of German universities,"[33] but he succeeded in creating a system of higher

---

[26] Slutsky, E., "Ein Beitrag zur formal-praxeologischen Grundlegung der Oekonomik," in *Zapiski Soziayalno-Ekonomitchnogo Vidilu*, vol. 4. Kiev, Ukrainian Academy of Sciences, 1926, pp. 238-249.

[27] Issaieff, A. A., "Schmollers Auseinandersetzung mit Smithianern und Marxianern," in *Die Neue Zeit*, vol. 16, # 32, 1897-98, p. 165.

[28] *Ibid.*, p. 167.

[29] *Ibid.*, p. 168.

[30] Epstein, M., *op. cit.*, p. 437.

[31] Brocke, B. v., "Hochschul- und Wissenschaftspolitik in Preussen und im Deutschen Kaiserreich 1882-1907: das "System Althoff," in *Bildungspolitik in Preussen zur Zeit des Kaiserreichs*, edited by P. Baumgart, Stuttgart, Klett Cotta, 1980, p. 27.

[32] *Ibid.*, pp. 47-52.

[33] *Ibid.*, p. 33.

education that was much admired throughout the world.[34] Harvard University, for example, honored Althoff with an honorary doctorate in 1906.[35] In Germany, Schmoller became one of Althoff's intimate advisers in recommending faculty appointments in the field of economics.[36]

Schmoller led an exhausting life, but he seems to have thrived on it. He exemplified the old adage: "Give the job you want done quickly and properly to a busy man and the job will be done properly." In addition to being a scholar (the German word is *Gelehrter*, a learned and erudite man), Schmoller remained an ardent social welfare state advocate for all his life. (Germans refer to him as a *Sozialpolitiker*.[37] For decades he fought against the left and the right. The left, led primarily by Marxists, wanted to revamp the existing social order according to Marx's precepts. These Marxists were intellectuals of many persuasions, but very few of them were workers themselves. They were self-appointed spokesmen for the working class. The right consisted mostly of laissez-fairists, who were mostly reactionaries. Schmoller wanted no bloody revolution but a step-by-step evolutionary process that would integrate the German masses into the mainstream of German society.[38] He served on numerous committees, drafted legislative proposals, was the tune-calling member of the *Verein für Socialpolitik*, and wrote memoranda for the German captains of industry and for high finance people. What emerges from Schmoller's multi-faced life is that economic ideas, methodological discussions, new forms of epistemology, and all activities must be made concrete in book or article form. For Schmoller, much of his effort also took the form of legislative proposals. Schmoller was either lucky or successful in that his work was disseminated widely via the book trade and through legislation. It must have been a source of satisfaction for Schmoller to see his decade-long work and advocacy of a better and more just life for the German working classes to come to fruition. Under Bismarcks's forceful leadership in 1883, Germany passed the *Sickness Insurance Law*. The *Accident Insurance Law* followed in 1884, and, in 1889, came the *Old Age and Disability Insurance Law*.[39] Schmoller dealt with the background and salient features of this legislation in his *Die Soziale Frage*.[40] There is no need to discuss Bismarck's motives for

---

[34] *Ibid.*, p. 46.

[35] *Ibid.*, p. 32.

[36] *Ibid.*, p. 70.

[37] Lütge, F., "Gustav von Schmoller als Sozialpolitiker," in *Schmollers Jahrbuch*, vol. 62, 1938, pp. 189-211.

[38] Franke, E., "Gustav Schmoller und die Sozialreform," in *Soziale Praxis und Archiv für Volkswohlfahrt*, vol. 26, # 44, 1917, p. 862.

[39] Kollermann, H. W., *Sozialpolitik in Deutschland. Eine geschichtliche und systematische Einführung*, 4th edition, Stuttgart, Kohlhammer, 1968, p. 43; see also Henning, H., "Sozialpolitik, III: Geschichte," in *Handwörterbuch der Wirtschaftswissenschaften*, vol. 6, 1977, pp. 94-95 and Fischer, W., *Handbuch der europäischen Wirtschafts- und Sozialgeschichte*, Stuttgart, Ernst Klett Verlag, 1985, pp. 435-436.

[40] The full title is: *Die soziale Frage. Klassenbildung, Arbeiterfrage, Klassenkampf*, München, Duncker & Humblot, 1918, pp. 118.

railroading this social legislation; the fact was that, in the 1880's, Germany under Bismarck was far ahead in the field of social welfare legislation.[41] Furthermore, American students flocked to German universities by the thousands, and Schmoller made a lasting impression on many of them. They returned to America with the idea that an economist must be able to link book knowledge and practical experience. German universities were "largely institutions designed to train men for the civil service in its various branches, being to this service a good deal what West Point and Annapolis are to our army and navy."[42] Many of these men later were founders of the American Economic Association in 1885.

By the turn of the century, Schmoller had become an important part of the German establishment of the *Second Reich*. He was elevated to the peerage in 1908; according to one report, Schmoller expressed misgivings about not having been consulted about this forthcoming honor. From then on, Schmoller was addressed as *His Excellency*.

The jubilee of Schmoller's seventieth birthday was celebrated with pomp and circumstance. He was honored with *three* Festschriften[43] and a collection of speeches.[44] Despite all the honors and decorations, Schmoller remained primarily an academic with a warm heart and a cool head, giving lectures and enjoying the preparations of his seminars. Admission to his seminar was difficult to obtain and it was considered a distinction to be selected.[45] The papers read at the seminar were of high level and Schmoller was a stern task master. But when he spoke his mind, his usual reserve melted away. One of his former American students, E. F. Gay wrote that Schmoller

> was oppressed by the mystery of the creative human spirit that moved behind the interlacing tangle of economics and social changes. Frequently at meetings of his seminar, after he had made one of his exciting suggestive commentaries on some student's paper, he would end, with an interweaving motion of his hands, by saying: *"Aber, meine Herren, es ist alles so unendlich compliziert."*[46]

---

[41] Crankshaw, R., *Bismarck*, New York, The Viking Press, 1981, p. 378.

[42] Ely, R. T., *Ground Under Our Feet*, New York, The Macmillan Company, 1938, p. 187.

[43] *Die Entwicklung der deutschen Volkswirtschaftslehre im neunzehnten Jahrhundert*, two volumes, Leipzig, Duncker & Humblot, 1908. *Grundrisse und Bausteine zur Staats- und zur Geschichtslehre*, ed. by K. Breysing et. al., Berlin, Georg Bondi, 1908. *Festschrift zu Gustav Schmollers 70. Geburtstag. Beiträge zur brandenburgischen und preussischen Geschichte*, Leipzig, Duncker & Humblot, 1908.

[44] *Reden und Ansprachen gehalten am 24. Juni 1908 bei der Feier von Gustav Schmollers 70. Geburtstag*. Nach stenographischer Aufnahme, Altenburg, 1908, 70 pp.

[45] Curtius, L., *Deutsche und antike Welt. Lebenserinnerungen von Ludwig Curtius*, Stuttgart, Deutsche Verlags-Anstalt, 1950, p. 134.

[46] Gay, E. F., "The Tasks of Economic History," in *Enterprise and Secular Change*, edited by F. C. Lane and J. C. Riemersma, Homewood, Illinois, R. D. Irwin, 1953, p. 411.

Translated into English it would mean, "But, gentlemen, everything is so incredibly complex." In his tireless efforts to understand the complicated nature of the social world, Schmoller was again suffering from the consequences of working like a beaver. Gay observed that his Professor was exhausted from the daily grind at the university, in government offices, on editorial boards, and by his own research. This mental fatigue, "enhanced (Schmoller's) tendency to aloofness from all except a small circle of family and friends."[47]

As years went by, Schmoller remained physically quite fit and mentally alert. Arthur Spiethoff, his assistant of many years, wrote that, according to Schmoller himself, "he had been seriously ill only once in his entire life."[48] That, of course, should be taken with a grain of salt. Since Schmoller worked under great pressure all his life, tension headaches plagued him. For instance, in the fall of 1905, in a letter to Max Weber, Schmoller wrote that the suffered so much from chronic neuralgic headaches that he could work for only a couple of hours in the evenings.[49]

Unlike Schmoller's vigorous participation in the *first Methodenstreit* during the 1880's, his participation during the *second* intellectual skirmish of his life over the problem of *Wertfreiheit* was not as forceful. Schmoller minced no words and said that a man could not live without values and that economics was not for the classroom but for the solution of pressing social problems. Of course, Max Weber and Werner Sombart assailed Gustav Schmoller's views on this matter and in so doing, made their academic reputations, but Schmoller was much more retiring after he reached the age of seventy. Yet he kept on working and refining his 'wirklichkeitsnahe Theorie' (realistic theory).[50] He also made sure that the process of social welfare legislation continued on course and that Germany's working masses slowly became an integral part of the society.[51] Theory for the theory's sake did not interest him at all! Schmoller continued to teach up to the ripe age of seventy-five, although, according to one Danish account, he had lost his magic touch in the lecture hall. Marstrand wrote that in the last days of July of 1911, when the heard Schmoller speak, it was a disappointment. By this time, Schmoller supposedly spoke in a feeble, at times barely audible voice.[52] He

---

[47] Anderson, *op. cit.*, p. 300.

[48] Spiethoff, A., "Gustav v. Schmoller," in *Schmollers Jahrbuch*, vol. 42, 1918, p. 27.

[49] Boese, F., *Geschichte des Vereins für Socialpolitik, 1872-1932*, Berlin, Duncker & Humblot, 1939, p. 116.

[50] Neuling, W., "Gustav Schmoller und die heutige Volkswirtschaftslehre," in *Finanzarchiv*, NF, vol. I, # 6, 1938/39, p. 369.

[51] Müssiggang, A., *Die soziale Frage in der historischen Schule der deutschen Nationalökonomie*, Tübingen, J. C. B. Mohr, 1968, p. 244.

[52] Marstrand, E., "Notitser. Gustav von Schmoller. (1838-1917), in *Nationaløkonomisk Tidsskrift,* vol. 55, 1917, p. 365. This obituary was translated from Danish into English by Finn B. Petersen of Laporte, Pennsylvania, USA.

4*

retired in 1912, but continued to give seminars until 1913.[53] Schmoller died on June 27, 1917, in Bad Harzburg, while on vacation.[54] The cause of death was aneurism.[55]

---

[53] Epstein, M., *op. cit.*, p. 435.

[54] Heubner, P. L., "Schmoller und der deutsche Westen," in *Kölnische Zeitung*, June 27, 1942.

[55] Hintze, O., Spiethoff, A., Beckerath, E. v., *op. cit.*, p. 338.

Chapter V

Schmoller's Grundriss: Its Salient Features and Critical Reception

Schmoller disliked intensely the hedonistic traits and the simplified versions of reality, cast in deductive mode, of the British and French classical economists. Almost from the very outset of his career, he strove to create a more realistic explanation of the social process of the German economy. He was reluctant to isolate the economic dimension from its related fields of law, politics, sociology, technology, art, and religion, even though he knew that such an isolation is necessary. Yet in his writing he practiced such isolation with great circumspection. In this respect, he was very much like his much admired Wilhelm Roscher who also isolated economic phenomena with even greater reluctance.[1]

Today, of course, economists, but particularly economic theorists, have no such inhibitions. They almost universally practice what the late Gunnar Myrdal once dubbed the "illegitimate isolation" of economic phenomena from social factors.[2] Schmoller believed that greater knowledge of economic history, supported by hard data from the German *Sozialstatistik*,[3] would lead to the emergence of the *Laws of Becoming* and thus supplement the classical *Laws of Being*.

This emerging broad based new economic science would to a great extent replace the existing, mechanistic and natural law-based economics, which lends itself so well for classroom use and which was so much respected by "armchair" academic economists. Schmoller felt that, for the time being, economic science did not yet have any hard and fast laws. And when such laws did emerge, he argued, even *then* the new economic science would be destined not for the classroom primarily but for the solution of pressing social and economic problems.

Was Schmoller moving in the direction of what today is known as *praxeology*, a general theory of purposeful action, anticipating the work of Eugene Slutsky in 1926 and of Ludwig von Mises?[4] Perhaps. However, for Slutsky and Mises

---

[1] Eisermann, G., *Die Grundlagen des Historismus in der deutschen Nationalökonomie*, Stuttgart, Ferdinand Enke Verlag, 1956, p. 139.

[2] Myrdal, G., *Asian Drama*, vol. 3, New York, The Twentieth Century Fund, 1968, p. 1535.

[3] Gorges, I., *Sozialforschung in Deutschland, 1872-1914*, Königstein/Ts., Verlag Anton Hain, 1980, pp. 104-120.

[4] Slutsky, E., "Ein Beitrag zur formal-praxeologischen Grundlegung der Oekonomik," in *Zapiski Soziayalno-Ekonomitchnogo Vidilu*, vol. 4, Kiev, Ukrainian Academy of

praxeology dealt with the means whereas for Schmoller the sole objective of his writing, working, teaching—in fact, his very existence—was designed to integrate the industrial masses, in the most peaceful way possible, into the mainstream of German society.[5] Schmoller sought ways and means for the strongest methods of influencing social and political life through the necessary social legislation.[6] In Schmoller's day, as well as today, academic economists have little interest in the solution of pressing social and economic problems. During his life, in England and France and even in a few universities in Germany, academic economists remained captives of the classical laws of economics, very much like today as most academic economists keep on "crunching the numbers." It is with this in mind, that in early 1987, the *London Economist* wrote that only one in twenty (1 : 20) academic economists takes any professional interest in the big questions of economic policy.[7] For Schmoller, the biggest social and economic challenge of the newly-created German Reich was the threat of the Marxist-inspired communism, which he called nothing but "centralistic despotism."[8] He wanted to cope with this menace to the existing social order by continuous social legislation, designed to improve the daily lot of the industrial workers. More than one hundred years ago, he pleaded for the creation of what today is known as the welfare state in West and East Germany, Scandinavian countries, and, with a much lower level of material comfort, even in the Soviet Union and other Eastern European countries. In a word, Schmoller probably did not care to be an economic theorist merely for the sake of being one. We, in our late twentieth century hindsight, have watched the bloodletting of the Soviet experimentation with some of the Marxist ideas. Maybe the time has come to give Schmoller at least the benefit of the doubt.[9]

With such a goal in mind, Schmoller collected archival materials and wrote statistical and economic *monographs* for almost twenty-five years of his academic career, from 1864 to 1887. Although his statistical material and methods seem coarse and lacking in sophistication today, we should not

---

Sciences, 1926, pp. 238-249. See also, Mises, L. v., *Human Action,* Chicago, Henry Regnery Company, 1966, p. 21, (Third Edition), where Mises wrote that "Praxeology deals with the ways and means chosen for the attainment of such ultimate ends. Its object is means, not ends."

[5] Müssiggang, A., *Die soziale Frage in der historischen Schule der deutschen Nationalökonomie,* Tübingen, J. C. B. Mohr (Paul Siebeck), 1968, p. 61.

[6] *Ibid.,* p. 118 and p. 239.

[7] *The Economist,* February 7, 1987, p. 84.

[8] Schmoller, G., *Grundriss der allgemeinen Volkswirtschaftslehre,* Munich and Leipzig, Duncker and Humblot, 1900, vol. I, p. 392.

[9] Maybe the new, more pragmatic leadership of the Soviet Union under Gorbatschow will undo the long decades of excessive Stalinist zeal and move the Soviet Union into a welfare state with more civil liberties and more material comfort for the average Ivan and Dunya. Maybe Schmoller's one-step-at-a-time program of a century ago deserves recognition after all?

underestimate the value of his persistent quest for empirical material. He craved numeric data and assiduously collected them throughout his academic life.

Schmoller also continually looked for new institutional material and for supporting evidence for the gradual change of these institutions over time. He wanted at all costs to avoid making the premature generalizations of the older German Historical School of Economics as represented, above all, by Wilhelm Roscher. During his tenure at the University in Halle and in Strassburg and even in the early years in Berlin, Schmoller indicated that for at least one generation economists should collect new institutional and statistical material and do mostly *descriptive* work before they ventured into generalizations.

Exhaustive detail, as Schmoller's American admirer, Thorstein Veblen, once claimed, was a necessary preliminary "to an eventual theory of economic life."[10] Schmoller did not study history for its own sake—not at all. For him, the study of history was a way to extract useful suggestions and lessons. He approvingly quoted Goethe, who once said

> Wer nicht von dreitausend Jahren
> sich weiss Rechenschaft zu geben,
> Bleibt im Dunkeln unerfahren,
> Mag von Tag zu Tage leben.

Paraphrased, in plain English, Goethe was saying that if someone does not know what went on for three thousand years, he/she remains basically ignorant, merely surviving from day to day.[11]

With such a long-term goal in mind, Schmoller and his students wrote many monographs. In Germany, there arose what might be called a tradition of monographs, which were considered stepping stones for eventual generalizations. For instance, the *Verein für Socialpolitik* initiated and financed 188 monographs, prior to its dissolution in 1932.[12]

Having spent more than two decades on "digging facts," that is, doing monographs, Schmoller eventually decided to perform a synthesis of his long labors. From the mid-1880's on, he spent all his efforts on a two-volume work which became known as *Grundriss*, for short. It is vital to keep in mind that the

---

[10] Veblen, T., "Gustav Schmoller's Economics," originally published in the *Quarterly Journal of Economics*, vol. 16, 1902, and reprinted in *The Place of Science in Modern Civilization and Other Essays*, New York, The Viking Press, 1930, p. 264.

[11] In a formal rendition, the above verse was translated as follows:
> He who cannot be far-sighted,
> Nor three thousand years assay,
> Inexperienced stays benighted,
> Let him live from day to day.

See, *West-Eastern Divan*, rendered into English by J. Whaley, London, Oswald Wolff Publishers, 1974, p. 91.

[12] Boese, F., *Geschichte des Vereins für Sozialpolitik, 1872-1932*, Berlin, Duncker & Humblot, 1939, pp. 305-322.

full title of it in German is *Grundriss der allgemeinen Volkswirtschaftslehre* and not a *Grundriss der allgemeinen Wirtschaftsgeschichte.*

Schmoller's *Grundriss* becomes, in translation, *An Outline of General Economics* and not an *Outline of General Economic History.* Throughout his life, Schmoller considered himself an economist, not a historian. He used chronicles, archival materials and applied historical methods in his writing, of course, but his aim was broad-based economics. Since the *Grundriss* has never been formally translated into English, perhaps a rough outline of its contents may be of service to the American readers.[13]

Volume I contains an Introduction (pp. 1-126) and two long parts called *books.* The Introduction consists of three chapters.[14] The first deals with what economics or political economy is all about and why economic phenomena must be isolated, with careful circumspection, from sociology, religion, law, technology, and art; the second chapter analyzes men's "herding tendencies" and the means of community life, such as custom, convention, morality, religion, and law.

This second chapter contains nine further sections. The *first* deals with the goals of the social community. The *second* section discusses the significance of speech, language, the written word, the importance of numbers, weights, and measures. In Schmoller's mind, all of the above constitute the psycho-physical apparatus of progress.

The *third* and *fourth* sections take up the mental sphere of consciousness and the collective components of the various communities where he distinguishes between the centripetal and centrifugal forces. The *fifth* section analyzes various human drives, such as pleasure and pain stimuli, self-preservation, desire for recognition, and competitive instincts. The *sixth* section focuses on acquisitiveness and economic virtues in general. Here Schmoller juxtaposes self-interest or egotism with greed and social injustice and suggests how to keep greed in proper bounds.

The *seventh* and *eighth* sections survey the ethical component of social life, its origin, evolution and the social means of sanction over time, be they the rule of thumb, custom, punishment by authority, religious remonstrance, or compulsion by law and order. The *ninth* section of the second chapter presents the interdependence between the natural and ethical elements of society on the one hand and the social institutions on the other. These nine sections run from pp. 6 to 76.

---

[13] The Library of Congress contains a mimeographed copy of a partially translated and paraphrased manuscript of Schmoller's Grundriss, vol. I, prepared in the fall of 1941 by Walter Abraham and Herbert Weingart, both students at Brooklyn College at that time, see its Preface.

[14] For a short summary of the contents of *Grundriss I,* see Farnam, H. W., "Schmoller's Grundriss," in *The Yale Review,* vol. 9, 1900/01, p. 167.

The *third* chapter (pp. 76-126) deals with the evolution of economic thought and economic methodology through time. It consists of five sections, in which Schmoller interprets the economic doctrines of the past. In the *third* section Schmoller's opening salvo is directed against the "invisible hand" doctrine of Adam Smith and his followers. The "invisible hand" supposedly created social harmony, all by itself. Schmoller depicted all such "natural law" explanations of "exchange societies," based on free, specializing individuals without much interference from the central government (p. 91), as veritable fairy tales. He felt it was childish to believe that the natural law ideas of Turgot, Quesnay, Smith, Ricardo, James and John Stuart Mill could be more than the first rudimentary attempts of a systematic science of economics (p. 93). Schmoller charged that classical economists did not pay enough attention to the historical causes and sources of British national wealth; they stressed only the almighty profit motive and virtually ignored the prevailing social institutions. Indeed, they isolated economic phenomena in their work too religiously and thus missed the significance of relationships among the law, government, religion, institutions, and culture (p. 99).

Nor did Schmoller like the economics of Karl Marx or other "scientific" socialist thinkers who were preaching open class struggle (pp. 97-99). Later on in the *Grundriss* he defined Marxian socialism as nothing but "centralistic despotism" (p. 392, p. 559). However, he took the Marxian challenge seriously. The remaining twenty-five pages of this chapter are devoted to methodology. Schmoller stressed the importance of abstraction for any meaningful observation (p. 101), and he called the reader's attention to the danger of *circular causation* (p. 107) in economics, something that the late Gunnar Myrdal used and repeatedly stressed in his *Asian Drama*.[15]

Furthermore, Schmoller pleaded with economists to use the procedure of isolation of economic variables from the rest of social phenomena with great circumspection. He posited (p. 110) that economic analysis must use simultaneously the institutional dimension, statistics, history, simplifications of reality in the form of a hypothesis or simple model, and, above all, psychology, which, in Schmoller's mind, provides the key to all the humanities.

In economics, Schmoller urged, both inductive and deductive methods are necessary (p. 110). But he went on to say that the "simpler sciences, like mathematics, mechanics, and astronomy, have already become almost completely deductive, whereas the simplest phenomena of economics do not lend themselves successfully to purely deductive treatment" (p. 111). Schmoller added that men who know reality are always a bit skeptical of deductive generalization; such people, he felt, crave to verify deductive generalizations.

To grasp the interdependence and multiple causes of social phenomena, Schmoller urged young economists to acquire knowledge of many fields,

---

[15] *Asian Drama*, p. 1846.

particularly those fields which are contiguous to economics proper (p. 112). To wit, an economist must know something about the law, constitution, and administration of the economy he is dealing with (p. 115). Finally, he urged young economists to travel, to learn languages, to conduct interviews and collect their own data, and only thereafter turn to the existing literature on a particular topic (p. 120).[16]

The long introduction leads us to Book I, which consists of four sections dealing with natural resources, people and population, and technology. The first examines the impact of natural conditions on people and their economies. Schmoller pays attention to the climate, topography, and water resources as the three factors which greatly influence all economies. He brings out the complex interactions among nature, culture, and evolving technology.

Section 2 covers different races and nationalities. Instead of postulating *Homo Oeconomicus*, Schmoller traces over time how the productive powers of different people produce, exchange and consume their outputs (pp. 141-160). Section 3 (pp. 160-190) takes up the population, its composition and changes over time. Here Schmoller presents hard-to-come-by data on sex, births and deaths of different people over many centuries. The fourth section of *Book One* traces the evolution of industrial arts from Stone Age to the end of the 19th century. He was particularly concerned with the influence of technology on the economic life of different people. Each subsection contains extensive bibliographical references in three languages—French, English, and German.

Book Two is entitled "Social Constitution of an Economy: Its Origin, Administration, and Contemporary Situation." It is divided into eight sections. The first, on the household economy (pp. 234-260), begins (as usual) with a large bibliography in three languages on the way households changed over time. Schmoller first surveys the evolution of the family up to the rise of matriarchy. Next follows a discussion of clans and the old patriarchal extended family. After the end of the period of barbarism, there is the emergence of *oikos*, the traditional household economy. Next, Schmoller sketches the salient features of the nuclear family, and makes a plea for the preservation of a strong family in the future.

Section two (pp. 260-284) deals with the rise of towns and cities from antiquity up to 1800. Having spent almost twenty years studying various archives, Schmoller offered a synthesis on this topic. The section also contains hard-to-come-by statistical data on urbanization in nineteenth century Europe and the USA.

---

[16] For comparison see W. Abraham and H. Weingast, *The Economics of Gustav Schmoller as Revealed in His Grundriss der allgemeinen Volkswirtschaftslehre*, Brooklyn, NY, Brooklyn College, 1942, mimeo, pp. 19-26 which deal with the *third* chapter of the Introduction.

Section three takes up the evolution of the public sector, with particular emphasis on the interaction among the family, municipality, and the central government (pp. 284-345). Schmoller wanted to know how the specific economic functions are distributed among the three sectors. He shows that the need to cope with the requirements of warfare and the obligation to provide police protection, adequate roads, and to support churches and education became the basic functions of the central government (p. 290). The government guarantees everyone a free field of economic activity, but the government also represents the collective economic interests of a given society (p. 291).

Schmoller offers (p. 291) a detailed list of government functions which differ considerably from those given by Adam Smith. He also stresses his belief that the doctrine of the "invisible hand" will not, by itself, provide a smoothly functioning government apparatus with orderly public finances (p. 292).[17]

It is in this long subsection that Schmoller makes his case for the creation of *social overhead capital* in the form of what today is known as *material infrastructure*. According to Schmoller, the central government builds and maintains roads, rivers, and ports in good operating condition (p. 322). Also, the central government provides for public health and education; this aspect of social overhead capital is known as *human infrastructure* (p. 337). Schmoller makes a strong case for a well-functioning *institutional infrastructure* in the form of an honest and efficient bureaucracy (p. 334).

Finally, Schmoller raises the question of the limits of public and private sectors in a given social order. He uses the example of private and corporate ownership of the means of production and parliamentary democracy of late nineteenth century Germany, with the Kaiser as a head of state. Schmoller advised that the public sector should not choke off the private sector. He insisted that the public and private sector should be in equilibrium; that the two sectors should correct each other constantly; that continuous expansion of government activity is not a blessing *without* corresponding progress of individual freedom and freedom of association. Schmoller concluded that England and the USA could afford to have a "weak government" and glorify the "laissez-faire" social order because these two countries had never been as threatened as Prussia had been. England is an island; the USA is protected by the Atlantic and Pacific Oceans.

The fourth section is an inquiry into the social and economic division of labor (pp. 346-396). Again, at the beginning of this section, Schmoller offers a two-page guide through the relevant literature in English, French, and German. He

---

[17] See Schmoller's revealing chapter on Prussia's bureaucracy, in *Umrisse und Untersuchungen zur Verfassungs-, Verwaltungs- und Wirtschaftsgeschichte besonders des Preussischen Staates im 17. und 18. Jahrhundert,* reprint, New York, Georg Olms Verlag, 1974, pp. 289-313.

never assumed that a knowledge of one language would be enough to analyze any problem of real importance.

This section deals with how labor and private property interact and bring about differentiation among human beings. The principle of the division of labor actually provides an explanation of the existing social and economic differences in societies. Schmoller presents a detailed discussion on the initial division of labor between man and woman in the family (p. 351). Then he gives an explanation of division of labor among the priests, warriors, chiefs, and traders. And finally, he describes the division of labor among the crafts, agriculture, and industry which gave rise to the wage labor class.

He packs this section with comparative statistical data on trade, industry, and agriculture in different countries in the nineteenth century. For Schmoller, unlike Adam Smith and the representatives of the free-trading Manchester School, division of labor (p. 392) was not a wonder of all wonders, a part of social harmony which comes about unconsciously, by the interacting, self-centered, profit-oriented, and isolated individuals. In other words, it was not a by-product of the "invisible hand."

For Karl Marx, division of labor was nothing but a byproduct of despotic anarchy of a market economy (p. 392). For Schmoller, on the other hand, division of labor was a *social process*, based on the unity of language, morality, customs, law, and administration. More precisely, division of labor as a social process constitutes a "battlefield" as well as a "community of co-operation in peace" (Friedensgemeinschaft) (p. 392). Division of labor is the great instrument of all progress, greater material well-being, and higher productivity. However, to provide social coherence, morality, and solidarity in an industrial society, you need not only specialists, but also men and women of general education (p. 395). A labor force with good general education, Schmoller claimed, can be retrained easily (p. 395).

The fifth section of Book Two examines the nature of property and its distribution (pp. 396-428). In thirty pages, Schmoller guides the reader through the early forms of property in terms of slaves and cattle (p. 399), property of nomads, and the land ownership patterns in the 19th century in the country and city. He also surveys the various theories of inheritance and private property.

The sixth section surveys the formation of social classes (pp. 428-455). It deals with the causes of class formation through time and stresses its psychological foundations. The seventh (pp. 456-496) section analyzes the emergence of the different forms of business enterprise through time. At the outset, Schmoller provides a four-page guide through the relevant literature on this subject in three languages. The concept of business enterprise, the appearance of the entrepreneur, and the origin of the profit motive are presented in terms of psychological, technological, and economic dimensions.

In the eighth section (pp. 496-560), Schmoller surveys the rise of the modern forms of enterprise and business organization. He deals with the emergence of the corporation (pp. 514-529), cooperatives (pp. 529-537), and cartels and trusts (pp. 537-551). Some of this material represents a synthesis of an Introduction and thirteen articles on the long-term evolution of the business enterprise which Schmoller published in his *Jahrbuch* in the 1890's and early 1900's.[18]

The first volume of the *Grundriss* was published in 1900, the second followed in 1904. The first consists of two parts, as we have seen, and the second volume contains books three and four and contains 833 pages. Incidentally, the two volumes together are 1393 pages long! The sheer bulk challenges the reader's patience and mind; two American economists once dubbed the *Grundriss* "elephantine."[19]

Book Three focuses on the social process of circulation and distribution of income, and consists of nine sections. The first (pp. 1-44) deals with the evolution of transportation and the changing nature of the market forms and trade patterns. Section 2 takes up the nature and functions of free competition and the evolving supervision of competitive forces over time (pp. 44-61), whereas section 3 surveys primarily the emergence of coinage, paper currency, and the impact of the money economy on social life and economics (pp. 61-105). Value and price are discussed in section 4 (pp. 105-185). Section 5 (pp. 185-239) discusses the national wealth concept, its statistical measurement, juxtaposes capital concept with that of credit, surveys the nature of interest, and discusses the evolution of usury.

Section 6 traces the nature, functions, and emergence of modern banking and its many forms (pp. 239-294). Section 7 (pp. 294-367) deals with the emergence of the wage earning class in modern times, industrial labor relations, determinants of wage levels, different wage theories, and the forces which determine the demand and supply of labor. Section 8 surveys the prevailing (around 1900) social institutions, such as different types of insurance, welfare, and labor union movements in different countries of the world (pp. 367-481). Section 9 (pp. 482-529) of Book Three of Volume Two takes up the distribution of income problem and surveys different types of income, such as profit and rent. It also gives figures for the distribution of Germany's national income for the year 1907 (pp. 490-495).

Book Four, called "The Evolution of Economic Life in General" consists of four sections. Its first section examines business cycles, their causes and various

---

[18] Selected fragments of these articles were translated into English and published as "The Historical Development of the Enterprise" in 1953; see *Enterprise and Secular Change,* edited by Lane, F. C. and Riemersma, J. C., Homewood, Illinois, R. D. Irwin, 1953, pp. 3-24.

[19] Ekelund, R. B. and Hebert, R. F., *A History of Economic Theory and Method,* New York, McGraw-Hill, 1975, p. 197.

"crashes" over time (pp. 530-562); section 2 (pp. 562-647) surveys the class struggle in space and time, with emphasis on class rule and changes brought about by government, law, and reform legislation. This section opens with an eight page bibliography in French, English, and German.

Section 3 (pp. 647-746) covers the economic relations and struggles among the various countries since the days of the old Greeks and Romans; it also deals with trade and tariff policies of various countries. The fourth and concluding section (pp. 746-775) deals with the economic and general evolution of humanity and individual nations. It ends with Schmoller's views of their rise and fall. A detailed subject and author index (pp. 776-833) concludes the *Grundriss*. After Schmoller had finished writing the *Grundriss II*, he admitted in the preface that he was "grateful" to fate for having witnessed its successful completion.[20]

The Grundriss: Difficult Reading Material

Very few contemporary economists have read the two volumes of Schmoller's treatise, line by line. Apart from linguistic difficulties in America,[21] *Grundriss* is not read in the German-speaking countries today either. For the past four decades German academic economists have been the most thorough emulators of the American academic economic theorists. No self-respecting West German academic economist would touch Schmoller's writings today.

Schmoller and his predecessors have long been judged harshly for the crime of "theoretische Knochenerweichung," as Professor Eisermann put it in 1956.[22] In English it would mean the theoretical "bone softening," or *osteomalacia* in medical terms. Yet as we celebrate his sesquicentennial birth, his work has been quietly read, evaluated, and rediscovered, and his legacy to the social scientists reappraised, more than two generations after his death, by the West German and a few American sociologists, historians, and political scientists. The tune-calling academic economists in both countries continue to shine in the academic halls and remain oblivious to the pressing social and economic problems of the day.

To evaluate any book, the reviewer always must pay attention to the method used and the new, additional knowledge it offers to a given field. Schmoller is always conceived by most economists to be a typical representative of the inductive method. Since he used a great deal of historical material and social statistics, he obviously used observation, integration, and analysis of his data.

---

[20] *Grundriss II*, p. V.

[21] Apart from the 73 page mimeographed, translated synopsis, called *The Economics of Gustav Schmoller as revealed in his Grundriss der allgemeinen Volkswirtschaftslehre*, by Walter Abraham and Herbert Weingast, Brooklyn College, 1942. The author used the copy of the Library of Congress.

[22] Eisermann, G., *Die Grundlagen des Historismus in der deutschen Nationalökonomie*, Stuttgart, Ferdinand Enke Verlag, 1956, p. 188.

But Schmoller did not reject deduction, only that deduction which rests on shallow, inadequate premises. In other words, Schmoller had less confidence in deduction than in induction. He felt that in broad-based economics, speculative deduction is not very helpful. He dealt with this problem at great length in the third chapter of the Introduction of the *Grundriss I*, especially in its fourth subsection. Schmoller walks on two methodological legs, but he limps a bit on the deductive leg.

Another methodological uniqueness of Schmoller is his refusal of neatly "factoring out" the economic phenomena and relegating all non-economic factors to the *ceteris paribus* cage. Schmoller analyzes all social phenomena in their setting and inter-dependence. His method of sensoring—to use the felicitious term of Professor Jürgen Backhaus—is to use simultaneously *six* different tools of analysis to deal with a particular problem.

In America, it was Wesley Clair Mitchell of Columbia University who once remarked that Schmoller treated his material from "four viewpoints,"[23] namely: historical evolution of any economic institution, statistics, theory, and "what ought to be done" about the problem under consideration. If one singles out relevant passages from the *first* volume of the *Grundriss*, one could, for instance, refer to p. 104, where Schmoller discusses the interaction of history, statistics, theory, and institutional factors. Schmoller declares, furthermore, that *Die Psychologie ist uns der Schlüssel zu allen Geisteswissenschaften und also auch zur Nationalökonomie*, which in English means that psychology is for us, the economists, the key to all humanities and hence to economics as well. Psychology is thus the often overlooked *fifth* tool of the Schmollerian broad-based economic analysis. The *sixth* tool of Schmoller's analysis is normative in nature of "what ought not to be".

For English-speaking economists, Schmoller's use of "ought to be's" in his economic analysis is completely unacceptable. It is a veritable mortal sin for an economist to wade into the "swamp" of normative economics. A long line of political economists from Ricardo and John Stuart Mill to Lionel Robbins made the doctrine of *value-free* economics supreme. It was Nassau W. Senior who laid down the rule that the "business of a political economist is neither to recommend nor to dissuade, but to state general principles..."[24]

John Neville Keynes (John Maynard's father), in 1890, differentiated among *positive economics, normative economics,* and *political economy.* According to him, "Political Economy is... a science, not an art or ethical inquiry. It is described as standing neutral between competing social schemes."[25] For Schmoller, the separation between *value-free positive economics* and *value-loaded political economy* was not clearly delineated.

---

[23] *Lecture Notes on Types of Economic Theory,* New York, A. M. Kelley, 1949, pp. 190-191.

[24] Senior, N. W., *An Outline of the Science of Political Economy,* London, 1836; reprinted by A. M. Kelley in New York, 1951, p. 3.

To settle the issue, and to eliminate political value judgments from economics, Max Weber wrote his well-known essay on the matter in 1903.[26] Weber's essay then gave rise to prolonged methodological controversies and became known as the *Werturteilstreit*; it ended with the victory of the Weber advocates of the *Wertfreiheit* in social sciences.[27] In the USA even today, for the most part, an economist considers himself to be "a neutral expert", and not an advocate.[28]

Schmoller had no inhibitions on this score. He was primarily concerned with the ways and means of improving the lot of the German industrial workers. He was not a hair-splitting, blackboard-using economic theorist; not at all. He was aiming to integrate the 'lower' classes into the mainstream of German society. He disliked, very much as John Maynard Keynes did a generation later, all Marxist social panaceas. He abhorred the Marxian vision of the future without any checks or balances, as the Stalinist experiences in the Soviet Union amply demonstrated a generation after Schmoller had died. His great ambition in life was the creation of the foundations for what today is the welfare state of West Germany and Northern European countries. It was this aspect of Schmoller's work that earned him the reputation for having "always been an advocate of what is called *state socialism* and a strong opponent of the doctrine of laissez-faire."[29] Welfare legislation in Schmoller's day, as it is now, had little or nothing to do with state socialism. Nor would Schmoller have had much use for the contemporary welfare economic theory. He was not interested in theory or Laws of Being, but in Laws of Becoming.

Schmoller's method of using simultaneously the six tools of economic analysis was used decades later in a somewhat different form by the renowned Joseph A. Schumpeter, who suggested that a *scientific economist* must use simultaneously economic theory, statistics, economic sociology, and economic history.[30] Throughout his life, Schumpeter adhered to the value-free stance in his work, even though he used the term *prognosis* in his *Capitalism, Socialism and Democracy* (1942). He left the impression that prognosis, in his case, was value-free.

Schmoller's style of multi-dimensional analysis and his unwillingness to isolate economic phenomena from the prevailing social setting had many

---

[25] Keynes, J. N., *The Scope and Method of Political Economy*, Fourth Edition, New York, Kelley and Millman, Inc., 1955, p. 13.

[26] Schön, M., "Gustav Schmoller and Max Weber," in *Max Weber and his Contemporaries*, London, Allen and Unwin, 1987, p. 67.

[27] Ferber, Christian v., „Der Werturteilstreit 1909/1959," in *Kölner Zeitschrift für Soziologie*, vol. 11, 1959, pp. 21-37.

[28] Nelson, R. H., "The Economics Profession and the Making of Public Policy," in *Journal of Economic Literature*, vol. 25, # 1, 1987, pp. 52-54.

[29] Farnam, H. W., "Schmoller's Grundriss," in *The Yale Review*, vol. 9, 1900-01, p. 173.

[30] Schumpeter, J. A., *History of Economic Analysis*, New York, Oxford University Press, 1954, pp. 12-16.

practitioners before him. As Jürgen Herbst wrote in his monograph twenty years ago, numerous German economists have stressed for a long time "the inseparability of economics, history, and political science."[31] It is this insight into the nature of the "mutual concatenation of all social phenomena"[32] at a particular time and place, and the emphasis on the circular causation and mutual inter-dependence or mutual conditioning that makes Schmoller's *Grundriss* difficult to digest. Apart from the difficulty of acquiring the necessary command of the various subfields Schmoller used, there is still another difficulty which makes his *Grundriss* an extremely challenging volume to read, to digest, and to use.

In *Grundriss II*, Book III, section 4 (pp. 105-185), Schmoller analyzes, among other things, the concept of demand and supply. He refuses to *isolate* price, as contemporary economists do, and to discuss the quantity responses in the case of a downward sloping demand curve, for instance. Such a procedure would constitute for Schmoller what Gunnar Myrdal calls the practice of "illegitimate isolation" of economic phenomena from the social setting.[33] The theoretical tradition of mainstream economics, in the past as well as today, considers such isolation of economic phenomena proper and indispensable. But Schmoller, even when discussing the law of demand and supply, still insisted that the idea of "circular causation" is at work and that monocausal explanation of price quantity relations is not quite proper.

For Schmoller, the demand curves can be downward as well as upward sloping. Unfortunately, Schmoller was either unwilling or unable to state clearly and precisely the general case of a downward sloping demand curve and thereafter to proceed to present the exceptions in a step-by-step fashion. Because Schmoller was aware of the time-lag in discussing supply curves, he included innumerable qualifications, which too often lose the reader. For the fledgling student of economics, this section must have been a nightmare. Such a student probably got a fever and switched his major. According to a story once heard in Göttingen, West Germany, Max Planck, the Nobel-prize winning physicist and the founder of *quantum physics*, felt that economics was much too difficult, and he turned to an easier subject, namely physics. This *Grundriss* chapter tries one's patience.

The wealth of material on prices and the problem of value over time are fascinating and instructive, but Schmoller does not provide a theory of price formation. As Wesley C. Mitchell once said, Schmoller failed to cement all the components he had presented. This lack of glue, or of an explanatory device is

---

[31] Herbst, J., *The German Historical School in American Scholarship. A Study in the Transfer of Culture*, Ithaca, N.Y., Cornell University Press, 1965, p. 18.

[32] Stark, W., *The History of Economics in its Relation to Social Development*, London, 1952, p. 6.

[33] Myrdal, G., *Asian Drama*, New York, The Twentieth Century Fund, 1968, p. 1535.

the greatest weakness of Schmoller's *Grundriss*.[34] It becomes obvious that Schmoller's text contains no micro-theory as economists understand the term today.

Schmoller's inability to do theoretical work can be demonstrated again by referring to *Grundriss* vol. 2, Book III, Section 2 (pp. 44-61) where he deals with the market structure known as pure competition. For the contemporary micro-theorist, pure competition means a particular market form, and he wants to know how a particular firm, called a price-taker, will make a profit or loss. To find out, the contemporary micro-theorist sets up a mathematical model. He writes the following equations:

1. $$C = aX^3 - bX^2 + cX + \bar{F}.$$

2. $$\bar{P} = \frac{dR}{dX}$$

3. $$\frac{dC}{dX} = \frac{dR}{dX}$$

4. $$R = P \cdot X$$

5. $$\pi = R - C$$

6. $$\frac{d^2C}{dX^2} \geq \frac{d^2R}{dX^2}$$

7. $$R \geq V$$

The first two are empirical equations. Equations 3, 4, and 5 are definitional equations, meaning that a purely-competitive firm will maximize profits by setting its marginal cost equal to marginal revenue. Number six is the necessary inequality to assure that we can find one output at which the purely competitive firm will maximize profits, provided we know the market price and the parameters of the cost function. Number seven is also an inequality to indicate the shut-down point of the purely competitive firm.

Of course, this chapter of Schmoller has none of such mathematical tools; instead, it is replete with comments on the abuses of pure competition by the economically strong who exploit the weak. It is a revealing chapter, full of learned and emotional vignettes, but it does not have the textbook simplicity, cast in mathematical mode, that static micro-theory offers to the fledgling student of economics today.

Even though Schmoller's presentation of the purely competitive market structure did not live up to the expectations of the contemporary mathematical economic theorist, it should be remembered that for Schmoller the science of economics had to include not only an analysis of *what exists*, but also a study of

---

[34] Mitchell, W. C., *Lecture Notes on Types of Economic Theory*, New York, Kelley, 1949, vol. 2, p. 193.

how economic life has come to be what it is. Stated differently, the deductive and hypothetical work of pure economic theorists deals with the laws of being, whereas Schmoller concentrated his efforts on discovering laws of tendencies. Unlike the "armchair academic economists" of the classical school and unlike the certainty and omniscience of the contemporary economic theorists, Schmoller was very cautious in his language and mode of expression. He probably was a typical "on the one hand, and, on the other hand" economist.

It is a pity that the recent attempt to cast the Mercantilist writers, Hume, Cantillon, Menger-Wieser into mathematical mode did not include the work of Schmoller![35] Even though Schmoller had such a profound grasp of the interdependence among economic variables as well as the existing concatenation among social phenomena, one looks in vain for a statement of general equilibrium, let us say, a là Walras. Nor does one find a method to deal with the interindustry flows from i to j industry, for a given period. There is no indication that Schmoller knew what the technical coefficients of production were. Hence there is no [A] matrix, no Leontief matrix, $[I-A]$ and no inverse of the Leontief matrix $[I-A]^{-1}$ in his work either. Even though Schmoller had an excellent analytical grasp of the interdependence of economic phenomena in a static situation and over time, his grasp was not an operational grasp. Contemporary economic theorists forever look for these tools in Schmoller's work. But, as repeatedly indicated, his emphasis was not on economic theory.

Critical Reception of the Grundriss Abroad and in Germany

The critical reception of *The Grundriss* was stormy. Part of the reason may lie in the *form* which Schmoller's *Grundriss* took. He supposedly wrote his text reluctantly. He had felt it would take three generations to assemble the material necessary for drawing conclusions (i. e., by the 1940's). Age was pressing on, and Schmoller felt compelled to analyze his assembled material. Edward F. Gay, Schmoller's American student, claims that the *Grundriss* was thus only a provisional outline, not a fully developed synthesis.[36]

Writing his *Grundriss* meant that Schmoller had to integrate whatever material he had on hand. It also meant that the time of economic analysis had arrived and the time for early preoccupation with economic history was receding into the background. Thus, the economic historian was turning into a "scientific economist," if one uses Schumpeterian, but not mathematical terms, doing simultaneously economic theory, statistics, economic sociology, and economic history. As noted above, Schmoller added two more dimensions to his analysis: psychology and policy implications.

---

[35] Brems, H., *Pioneering Economic Theory, 1630-1980. A Mathematical Restatement,* Baltimore, The Johns Hopkins University Press, 1986, p. 12.

[36] Gay, E. F., "The Tasks of Economic History," in F. C. Lane and J. C. Riemersma (eds.), *op. cit.,* Homewood, Ill., R. D. Irwin, 1953, p. 410.

5*

Critical Reception in the USA and UK

Immediately upon the appearance of the first volume of the *Grundriss* in 1900, an American professor, Edwin R. A. Seligman, wrote a review saying that this work has been "constructed on lines so different from those to be found in English literature."[37] Seligman did not like Schmoller's nationalism; he called it "the prevalent chauvinism of the Germans." He suggested that the volume did not quite do what it promised. The science of economics must include, Seligman wrote, "not only an analysis of what exists, but also a study of how the economic life has come to be what it is."[38] According to Seligman, the English economists have concentrated on *what exists*, whereas Schmoller directed his efforts on how economic life has come to be what it is.

In the process, Seligman argued, Schmoller lost sight of what exists, that is, he de-emphasized economic theory and its role in economic analaysis. Seligman felt that the political economy of future generations will be a combination of Schmoller and Ricardo. He wrote: ". . . we cannot have any science worthy of the name without the deductive and hypothetical work of the so-called 'pure theorists'; but it will at the same time confess that the laws of economic life comprise not only the *laws of being*, but also the *laws of becoming*, and that the historical generalizations of Schmoller are essential, although not adequate, to a thorough comprehension of actual conditions."

Schmoller had accomplished an enormous task, Seligman conceded, but he gave theory short shrift, and his "so-called Outline of Economics had very little in common with what is usually termed economic science."[39] The *Grundriss* contains "not the principles of political economy, in the form of an analysis of the problem of value, but rather the principles of economic development and the relations of economic to social life."[40] In sum, Seligmann felt that Schmoller did not have any real conception of what pure economic theory is all about.

Professor Henry W. Farnam, Schmoller's student who lodged in his house at Strassburg during the 1870's, also reviewed his master's *Grundriss I* shortly after its publication. To evaluate this work, Farnam asked three basic questions: What was the scientific method used? In what manner has the author put his methodological views into execution; and what were the additions to knowledge that emerged from this new work?[41]

Farnam stressed that Schmoller used both the deductive and inductive methods, but the difference between Schmoller and the English, French, and

---

[37] For Seligman's review, see *Political Science Quarterly*, vol. 15, # 4, 1900, p. 728.

[38] *Ibid.*, p. 732.

[39] *Ibid.*, p. 730.

[40] *Ibid.*, p. 731.

[41] Farnam, H. W., "Schmoller's Grundriss," in *The Yale Review*, vol. 9, 1900-01, p. 166.

Austrian economists was "one of proportion and emphasis, not of essence."[42] According to Farnam, Schmoller approached the making of generalizations and the framing of economic laws "with extreme caution." The concatenations of the *Grundriss I*, with its continuous swings back and forth into the fields of history sociology, geography, meteorology, ethnology, and technology, did not escape Farnam.[43] The reviewer was impressed with the broad scholarship of his former mentor and his ability to assimilate his vast knowledge into one volume.[44] But Farnam was afraid that Schmoller over-extended himself by covering so many subfields of social sciences and that he was liable to errors which "will be detected by specialists."[45]

Farnam particularly liked the chapter on the role of government in economic life and the chapter on the division of labor. However, Farnam did not like Schmoller's habit of using derogatory epithets and expressions regarding some economists and their opinions, which at times creates the impression that Schmoller is intolerant. Farnam also felt that Schmoller had a "tendency to overrate the importance of purely descriptive monographic work."[46] Despite many reservations, Farnam felt, however, that "for one who desires a comprehensive review of economic history and of the growth af economic institutions in the evolutionary spirit, no better work can be found than the present volume."[47]

Alas, concluded Farnam, "it is not possible at the present time to estimate the positive advance in economic theory which Professor Schmoller's book will make, because the theoretical part is still to come."[48] It was Farnam's way of saying that the *Grundriss I* de-ephasized pure economic theory. Nevertheless, in Farnam's view Schmoller had rendered "most important services...to economic science."[49]

Another American, Thorstein Veblen, called the publication of the *Grundriss I*, "an event of the first importance in economic literature."[50] It was to him a "compendious statement" of Schmoller's theoretical position and exemplification of the scope and method of economic science. Veblen considered Schmoller to be "an economist who is...an innovator, not to say...an iconoclast," whose treatise "...touches the foundations ot the science...intimately and profound-

---

[42] *Ibid.*, p. 167.

[43] *Ibid.*, p. 168.

[44] *Ibid.*, p. 170.

[45] *Ibid.*, p. 171.

[46] *Ibid.*, p. 173.

[47] *Ibid.*, pp. 170-171.

[48] *Ibid.*, p. 173.

[49] *Ibid.*, p. 174.

[50] Veblen, T., "Gustav Schmoller's Economics," in *The Place of Science in Modern Civilization and other Essays*, New York, The Viking Press, 1930, p. 252.

ly..."[51] Veblen pointed out that Schmoller wanted "to formulate a body of economic theory on the basis afforded by the 'historical method,'"[52] something hitherto not yet seriously attempted. He went on to say that Schmoller's *Grundriss I* represented a "branch of historical economics which professes to cultivate theoretical inquiry."[53]

In Veblen's view, Schmoller had modernized the historical school of economics and it had "passed from a distrust of all economic theory to an eager quest of theoretical formulations."[54] Veblen also suggested that Schmoller's numerous monographs, as well as his partiality to exhaustive detail, are the necessary preliminaries to an eventual theoretical explanation of economic life and institutional change. These preliminaries can pave the way for a formulation of social laws of causation, or the *laws of becoming over time*. In this effort, meticulous historical investigations, stressing the evolution of social and economic institutions, play a large part, but not the sole part, Veblen pointed out.[55]

In Veblen's mind, the salient feature of the *Grundriss I*, was the "post-Darwinian causal theory of the origin and growth of species of institutions."[56] Veblen applauded Schmoller's unique arrangement of the material presented; he claimed that the "significant innovation" of the work lay not in the mass of details but in the presentation of how the economic situation had arisen by a cumulative process of change. Veblen liked Schmoller's multi-dimensional method of analysis of the emergence of economic and social institutions over time, but he firmly rejected Schmoller's habit of giving the reader his advice of what to do about this or that problem. Veblen had no use for Schmoller's normative values; he also disliked Schmoller's treatment of the "woman question," his treatment of the family, and his characterizations of "half-civilized" and "civilized" nations. But on the whole, Veblen wrote, *Grundriss I* was, despite these shortcomings, "a work of the first magnitude."[57] Was it love at first sight?

In England, *Grundriss I* received a favorable review in the prestigious *Economic Journal*. The reviewer said Schmoller's volume deserved "the closest attention" of the economics profession.[58] The reviewer also liked Schmoller's method of treating "economic life as one side of a common social life,"[59] but he

---

[51] *Loc.cit.*

[52] *Ibid.*, p. 254.

[53] *Ibid.*, p. 256.

[54] *Ibid.*, p. 256.

[55] *Ibid.*, p. 264.

[56] *Ibid.*, p. 265.

[57] *Ibid.*, p. 278.

[58] Gonner, E. C. K., in *Economic Journal*, vol. 11, 1901, p. 220.

[59] *Ibid.*, p. 222.

stressed that economic analysis suffers when economic factors are not isolated. He also felt that Schmoller's method "may lead to wide rather than careful detailed knowledge."[60]

Critical Reception in Germany

As expected, Schmoller's *Grundriss I* received numerous reviews in his native Germany. For instance, Alexander Meyer emphasized that the *Grundriss I* contained material not usually found in an economics text. He called it "a beautiful book," but he disagreed with everything it contained, from the first to the last word.[61] Meyer disliked Schmoller's habit of stressing that an individual is a dependent individual, not an isolated individual a là Adam Smith. He complained that Schmoller had nothing to offer on human liberty and individualism.[62] He felt that Schmoller deliberately subjugated the individual to the will of the government authority and thus narrowed the freedom of the individual. Having rearranged the traditional subjects of economics in Schmoller's way, Meyer felt that this was an unacceptable and unscientific way to proceed in an economics treatise.[63]

The reviewer also charged that the *Grundriss I* did not teach the reader how to develop the capacity to think and do synthesis. The salient feature of the *Grundriss I*, according to Meyer, was the justification of the government to interfere with the economic life of a nation.[64] Finally, Meyer singled out Schmoller's emphasis on the strong relationship between history and economics. In a nutshell, in Meyer's mind, the *Grundriss I* was an encyclopedia of social sciences, admirably done, but it was not an economics textbook.[65]

Professors Karl Diehl and Wilhelm Hasbach reviewed the first volume of the *Grundriss* in 1902. Diehl praised it for its wealth of data and called it a highly useful and valuable work.[66] He was particularly impressed with Schmoller's method of presenting economic life as a part of the entire culture of a given society. *Grundriss I* is much more comprehensive than the usual economics text. Schmoller's analysis was multidimensional, Diehl argued, for he had skillfully

---

[60] *Ibid.*, p. 223.

[61] Meyer, A., "Schmoller's Volkswirtschaftslehre," in *Die Nation*, vol. 18, 1900-01, p. 68. Left aisle.

[62] *Ibid.*, p. 68, left aisle.

[63] *Ibid.*, p. 68, left aisle.

[64] *Ibid.*, p. 69, left aisle.

[65] *Ibid.*, p. 68, right aisle.

[66] Diehl, K., "Über die nationalökonomischen Lehrbücher von Wagner, Schmoller, Dietzel und Philippovich mit besonderer Rücksicht auf die Methodenfrage in der Sozialwissenschaft," in *Jahrbücher für Nationalökonomie und Statistik*, vol. 3, # 24, 1902, p. 107.

used the various subdisciplines of economics. The reviewer praised as masterful Schmoller's method of integrating his encyclopedic knowledge.

However, noted Diehl, "books like people suffer from deficiencies of their virtues...,"[67] and Schmoller was no exception. Diehl feared that the mass of detail might confuse the beginning student of economics who would not see the essential relationship of economic life. Such confusion could result, he said, because Schmoller had deliberately eliminated the conventional theoretical tools from this work. Schmoller refused to employ the rationalistic abstractions of classical economics without reference to the ethical, legal, national, and religious factors of a given society; Schmoller believed that without such references genuine economic knowledge was impossible.[68]

Diehl himself had strong theoretical preferences, and he took Schmoller to task for disregarding the existing analytical apparatus of British classical and neo-classical economics. He argued that psychology is an insufficient tool, no matter how well integrated with other subdisciplines of economics. Despite numerous objections to Schmoller's treatise, Diehl emphasized that "only a certain part of economics can properly use the so-called method of isolating strictly economic phenomena from other dimensions of social life."[69] Furthermore, in *Grundriss I* Schmoller had softened his early, rigid stand on methodology; he was now willing to admit that deduction and induction supplement each other.

The other reviewer of 1902, Wilhelm Hassbach, considered *Grundriss I* as the "first foundation (Grundlegung) of political economy from the historical point of view."[70] Schmoller's two-decade long preliminary work in the field of economic history, social statistics, sociology, ethics, and philosophy had all been integrated into the treatise. In Hasbach's estimation, *Grundriss I* represented "definite progress" in the field of economics.

Schmoller had always rejected the idea that self-interest is the only real motive of economic life, and he was apprehensive about the exploitation of the economically weak by the economically strong and powerful elements of the German society. Hasbach was particularly attracted by Schmoller's ability to present an analysis of the relationship among government, law, custom, and the economy.[71] He felt that Schmoller's use of psychology was quite novel in an economics principles text. Furthermore, Schmoller's analysis of the different forms of governmental structure enabled him to recognize the typical and recurring phenomena of the economic process; whether they are dubbed as laws

---

[67] *Loc.cit.*

[68] *Loc.cit.*

[69] *Ibid.*, p. 132.

[70] Hasbach, W., "Gustav Schmoller, Grundriss der allgemeinen Volkswirtschaftslehre," in *Jahrbücher für Nationalökonomie und Statistik*, vol. 23, 1902, p. 387.

[71] *Ibid.*, p. 394.

of evolution or "hypothetical truth" is immaterial. What matters is that these concepts can serve as instruments of insight into the creation of efficient government structures.[72]

In Hasbach's mind, the publication of *Grundriss I* was an event very much like the publication of the *Wealth of Nations* 125 years earlier.[73] Hasbach was certain that Schmoller's treatise would guide future generations of economists for a long time to come.

In 1908, the Austrian economist Karl Th. von Inama-Sternegg, in a long review of the *Grundriss*, appreciated Schmoller's multi-dimensional presentation of the subject but felt that his attempts to reduce the economic behavior of human beings to their physiological, psychological, and ethical roots was an aberration in social research.[74] This field of inquiry did not belong to the legitimate field of inquiry for an economist, he wrote. Inama-Sternegg went on to say that the first part of Schmoller's *Grundriss I* would not exactly appeal to academic economists or to business economists.[75]

The publication of *Grundriss II* in 1904 evoked another wave of flattering, contradictory and rejecting responses. For instance, in England, the home of economic science, the second volume of the *Grundriss* was again favorably reviewed by E. C. K. Gonner, but he felt that the "weak point lies . . . on the side of abstract analysis."[76] But he liked very much Schmoller's massive assault on the crude, simplistic, and mechanistic theories, which, in the past, had failed to deal properly and adequately with the complex nature of society.[77] He felt that the value of the *Grundriss* could hardly be over-estimated.

In Germany, Professor Karl Diehl wrote that a careful perusal of it would offer a "rewarding lesson"[78] because of its enormous scope. Yet, Diehl disliked Schmoller's habit of reducing all economic phenomena to their supposed psychological roots. Similarly, as in *Grundriss I*, the theoretical part dealing with the problem of production and distribution had neglected the theoretical groundwork of British classical economists.[79]

In conclusion, Diehl noted the great paradox of Schmoller's work: this major treatise of the ethico-historical school of economics, whose main aim was to destroy the natural laws of the Classical School of Economics, had in fact,

---

[72] *Ibid.*, p. 394.

[73] *Ibid.*, p. 403.

[74] Inama-Sternegg, K. Th. v., *Neue Probleme des modernen Kulturlebens*, Leipzig, Verlag von Duncker & Humblot, 1908, p. 110.

[75] *Ibid.*, p. 119.

[76] *Economic Journal*, vol. 16, 1906, p. 263.

[77] *Ibid.*, p. 264.

[78] Diehl, K., "Gustav Schmoller, Grundriss der allgemeinen Volkswirtschaftslehre," in *Jahrbücher für Nationalökonomie und Statistik*, vol. 29, 1905, p. 234.

[79] *Ibid.*, p. 235.

established a new type of natural law theory. British classical economists explained economic phenomena by invoking the application of self-interest, whereas Schmoller used a number of natural instincts to explain different social institutions and their transformation over time.[80] Diehl felt that Schmoller's work was based in many ways on Herbert Spencer's work, incredible as it may sound. In a nutshell, *Grundriss II*, like *Grundriss I*, was not yet a treatise in economic theory.

A few years later, Georg von Below, wrote a devastating review of the Schmoller work. Since the review represented a total rejection of what Schmoller stood for, it will be stated in the German language first and a translation will follow. In German, G. v. Below wrote as follows:

> Wollte man Schmollers Darstellung wirklich berichtigen, so müsste man ein doppelt so dickes Buch wie das, das er verfasst hat, schreiben, denn gerade bei seiner weichen, unbestimmten Art ist das Korrigieren nicht einfach. Mein Zweck war, zu zeigen, von welcher Art sein vielgerühmtes 'Historisches Material' ist. Die Quantität ist unbestreitbar. Der Fehler liegt jedoch in der Qualität... Er hat seinen grossen Ruhm — neben seiner mehr praktisch-politischen Agitation — namentlich dem Umstand zu verdanken, dass die Historiker Respekt vor dem Nationalökonomen, die Nationalökonomen vor dem Historiker haben zu müssen glaubten, es wirkt dann befreiend, wenn man sich klar macht, dass er eine spezifisch wissenschaftliche Kraft überhaupt nicht ist. In den Prinzipienfragen ist er nicht klar, in der Quellenbenutzung willkürlich.[81]

The above in the English translation means:

> If one really wanted to correct Schmoller's presentation, one would have to write a book twice as long as the one he produced, since it is precisely his soft, uncertain manner which makes correction a not so simple task. It was my purpose to demonstrate the nature of his much-applauded 'historical material.' The quantity cannot be denied. However, the defect lies in the quality. Except for his more practical-political actions, he owes his great fame primarily to the circumstance that historians believed that they owed respect to the political economist, and the political economists believed that they owed respect to the historian; and it is liberating to finally realize that he isn't a specifically scientific talent at all. In questions of basic principles he is unclear, in the employment of sources arbitrary.

Schmoller's *Grundriss* is a concoction, "drawn from many sources without being synthesized into a coherent system,"[82] as Professor Frederic C. Lane put it in 1956. Below dubbed the *Grundriss* an eclectic work and eclecticism is supposedly bad. Lane also noted that Schmoller "disparaged theory and extolled historical research."[83]

---

[80] *Ibid.*, p. 236.

[81] Below, G. v., "Wirtschaftsgeschichte innerhalb der Nationalökonomie," in *Vierteljahresschrift für Sozial- und Wirtschaftsgeschichte*, vol. 5, 1907, p. 521.

[82] Lane, F. C., "Some Heirs of Gustav von Schmoller," in *Architects and Craftsmen in History. Festschrift für Abbott Payson Usher*, Tübingen, J. C. B. Mohr, (Paul Siebeck), 1956, p. 11.

In America, Schmoller's former student at the University of Strassburg who had become Professor of Economics at Yale University, reviewed also the second volume of the *Grundriss*.[84] Farnam argued that Book Three contained an analysis of "strictly economic laws," whereas the rest of the volume was "devoted to the description of social institutions or the discussion of problems of history and governmental policy."[85] The entire work was characterized by "fullness of detail," and Farnam felt that "the strong point of the book lies in the description of great social institutions and social movements..."[86]

Schmoller was not particularly fond of American-style democracy nor did he care for the prevailing American institutions. He believed, all his life, "in the ability of a sovereign or a group of statesmen standing above class interests to regulate wisely and harmoniously the conflicting claims of social groups."[87] Farnam did not like Schmoller's views of America and its social institutions and scoffed at his occasional and hasty generalizations. Nevertheless, Farnam expressed admiration "for the learning and the genius which have made it possible for [Schmoller] to cover in one harmonious and systematic work such an enormous range of anthropological, geographical, technical, statistical, philosophical, and historical material..."[88]

In Tsarist Russia, the two volumes of the *Grundriss* received a thorough review in 1907. The reviewer, R. G. Voblyj, did not like the method used by Schmoller, nor did he appreciate the relativism of the German Historical School of Economics. Such limitations represented for him a kind of *testimonium paupertatis* of Schmoller's economics.[89] He gave a full account of the contents of the two volumes and made a running commentary on each chapter praising and critiquing. Voblyj's particular praise went to Schmoller's discussion of free competition and the evolution of the monetary economy.[90] But he rejected Schmoller's method of welfare policy via legislation as the best method to improve the lot of industrial workers.[91] He also took Schmoller to task for not understanding the materialistic interpretation of history.[92] In Voblyj's mind, Schmoller's *Grundriss* represented not a theory of political economy but its

---

[83] *Loc. cit.*

[84] Farnam, H. W., "Grundriss der Allgemeinen Volkswirtschaftslehre. Von Gustav Schmoller. Zweiter Theil. Leipzig, Duncker und Humblot, 1904, pp. x, 719," in *The Yale Review*, vol. 14, 1905, pp. 216-218.

[85] *Ibid.*, p. 217.

[86] *Ibid.*, p. 218.

[87] *Loc.cit.*

[88] *Loc.cit.*

[89] Voblyj, R. G., review in *Zhurnal Ministerstva Narodnogo Prosveshcheniya*, vol. 7, #2, 1907, p. 367.

[90] *Ibid.*, p. 372 and p. 373.

[91] *Ibid.*, p. 378.

[92] *Ibid.*, p. 380.

history. He cited Dietzel in support of his conclusion: even though the German Historical School of Economics had tried to destroy the foundations of the British classical school of economics, it had not been able to create a new theoretical foundation.

Reaction to the Dominance of Schmoller's School in Germany

Yet it was the inadequacy of Schmoller's realistic economic theory that made a number of German economists uneasy. Ludwig Pohle, for instance, wrote in 1911[93] that the German Historical School of Economics had actually destroyed real economic theorists. The one-time president of the School of Business of Berlin, Moritz Bonn, also deplored the fact that the German Historical School of Economics perverted the German bureaucracy and that hardly anyone in the Reich's Finance Ministry had any ideas of what inflation was. Supposedly, Schmoller's students were taught to look backwards, not into the future.

To improve matters, in 1913, a new German periodical, *Weltwirtschaftliches Archiv*, still extant, was launched as a counterforce against Schmoller's historical school of economics.[94] In its first issue, Bernhard Harms, the first director of the Institut für Weltwirtschaft, located in Kiel, criticized Schmoller for his contradictory concept of a national economy. The new periodical was designed to stimulate theoretical work in international economics. Even today, it is a world-renowned journal in that field.[95]

At the time of his death, Schmoller was still acclaimed by many for his *Grundriss*, based on sound scholarship, wide reading, mature judgment, and fine style.[96] However, a memorial essay by Adolf Braun declared him neither a scholar of political economy or history, but merely an influential politician.[97] The writer of the essay felt that, in the long run, Schmoller's influence on political economy will be insignificant.[98]

In 1918, shortly after his passing, Imperial Germany sued for peace. The huge reparations bill presented to the defeated Germans led to hyper-inflation, which virtually destroyed the German middle-class and, in many ways, paved the way for Hitler and the Third Reich. Had the Germans been able to pay the imposed reparations, they would have been doing so until 1988! Today it is almost universally forgotten what young John Maynard Keynes wrote in his *The*

---

[93] Pohle, L., *Die gegenwärtige Krisis in der deutschen Volkswirtschaftslehre,* 1911.

[94] "Weltwirtschaft und Weltwirtschaftslehre. (Zugleich als Einführung in das Archiv.)" in *Weltwirtschaftliches Archiv,* vol. 1, 1913, p. 7.

[95] The library of the Institut für Weltwirtschaft, with its unique, four-dimensional catalogue has no peers in the entire world even today.

[96] Epstein, M., "Obituary. Gustav Schmoller," in *Economic Journal,* vol. 27, 1917, p. 426.

[97] Braun, A., "Gustav Schmoller," in *Die Neue Zeit,* vol. 35, # 2, 1917, p. 378.

[98] *Ibid.,* p. 383.

Economic Consequences of the Peace, in 1919, and in his *Memoir on Melchior,* published posthumously in 1949, wherein he pleaded for a sane, not impossible, reparations policy.

Alas, since the Allies were not as magnanimous to Germany after World War I as they were after World War II, the country went through the whirlpool of hyper-inflation, destruction of the German middle-classes, and radicalization of German society. Yet since the word "inflation" was not in the subject index of the *Grundriss,* Schmoller was castigated for his supposed neglect of the mechanics of inflation and social consequences of hyper-inflation, in particular.[99] Had the above-cited author looked more carefully, he would have found much material on this subject under the heading of *Geldwertveränderungen.*[100] In any event, as hyper-inflation raged unchecked during the years of 1922 and 1923, the *Grundriss* was found to be useless.

After the end of World War I and for the next two decades, the *Grundriss* was being reviewed and scrutinized. For instance, Carl Brinkmann was favorably impressed by Schmoller's mastery of the various sub-fields of economics. He called it encyclopedic in scope, a summary of previous monographic efforts.[101] Even though the work fell short in its theoretical parts, Schmoller's treatise was actually a text of economic aspects of social process, he stated and, for this reason, Schmoller was actually a sociologist, even though he considered himself an economist and historian. Brinkmann wrote in 1937 a long chapter on Schmoller's *Grundriss* and praised it for its unique emphasis on the entire social process.[102]

Surely, Schmoller did not use the methods of Walras's or Cassel's general equilibrium analysis, but Schmoller's merit was that he *did not isolate* the demand and supply factors, the process of production and distribution from the rest of the society[103] or from the ongoing social process. Brinkmann noted that Schmoller's analysis of the demand factors in *Grundriss II* (p. 136) contained a much needed preliminary analysis of a household, and praised Schmoller's analysis of the firm and his discussion of interest, rent, and wages. Brinkmann also rejected Edgar Salin's claim that Schmoller's work represented an aberration of theoretical research in economics.[104]

---

[99] Professor Dr. R. W., "Gustav Schmoller. Zum 100 Geburtstag am 24. Juni," in *Berliner Tageblatt,* June 24, 1938.

[100] The interested reader might also be interested in Schmoller's essay on this topic, "Neuere Arbeiten über Geldwertveränderungen und neuere Preissteigerungen," published in 1912.

[101] Brinkmann, C., "Schmoller's Grundriss," in *Weltwirtschaftliches Archiv,* vol. 17, 1921/22, p. 90.

[102] Brinkmann, C., *Gustav Schmoller und die Volkswirtschaftslehre,* Stuttgart, Verlag W. Kohlhammer, 1937, p. 174.

[103] *Ibid.,* p. 175.

[104] *Ibid.,* p. 173.

In 1923, Salin wrote the *Geschichte der Volkswirtschaftslehre.*[105] In this work, Salin spoke of Schmoller's "pernicious influence" in German economics. He considered Schmoller to be a scholar who had written a number of good monographs but claimed Schmoller had no talent for theoretical work and for this reason was actually a destroyer of German economics.[106] In the previous year, Salin had chastized Schmoller for his methodological one-sidednes,[107] and compared the *Grundriss* to a gigantic mountain—impossible to conquer.[108] In his view, Schmoller was incapable of doing any real theoretical work and he wrote primarily in a descriptive manner.[109] Salin wondered if anyone would ever read the *Grundriss* and of what value it would be.

These turned out to be foreboding questions. In a word, Schmoller was supposedly the un-doing of German theoretical economics. After the publication of Salin's book in 1923, Schmoller's successor in Berlin, Professor Heinrich Herkner, accused Salin of being guilty of splitting hairs and condemning, unjustly, Schmoller's efforts at synthesis.[110] Ironically, Salin's lifetime work did not measure up to his early theoretical ambitions.

But as time went on, German economists felt more and more inclined to say that Schmoller tried to cover too many subfields of economics and that, basically, he remained an historian.[111] The great Austrian economist Carl Menger once charged that Schmoller was doing "historische Mikrographie"; Schmoller, he felt, was a man who did not quite understand that empirical research and theoretical analysis were two quite different activities of an economist.

Schmoller's student Werner Sombart once noted that it was simply amazing how much material the two volumes of the *Grundriss* contained. He called the work a gigantic *specimen eruditionis,* but feared that it would soon fall into oblivion.[112] Schmoller's *Grundriss,* said Sombart, was oppressing and confusing instead of edifying and stimulating because it lacked "an ordering and organizing idea," i.e., an hypothesis. However, Sombart praised Schmoller's

---

[105] Salin, E., *Geschichte der Volkswirtschaftslehre,* Third edition, Bern, Verlag A. Francke, 1944, p. 3.

[106] *Ibid.,* p. 3.

[107] *Schmollers Jahrbuch,* vol. 45, 1922, pp. 483-505.

[108] Salin, E., *Geschichte der Volkswirtschaftslehre,* third edition, Bern, Verlag A. Francke, 1944, p. 171.

[109] Salin, E., "Zur Stellung G. Schmollers in der Geschichte der Nationalökonomie," in *Schmollers Jahrbuch,* vol. 48, 1924, p. 311.

[110] Herkner, H., "Zur Stellung G. Schmollers in der Geschichte der Nationalökonomie," in *Schmollers Jahrbuch,* vol. 47, 1924, p. 8.

[111] Erb, O., "Gustav von Schmoller. Zum hundertsten Geburtstag," in *Frankfurter Zeitung,* June 24, 1938.

[112] Sombart, W., "Gustav Schmoller, 1838-1938," in *Der deutsche Volkswirt,* July 1, 1938.

attempts to get away from the pure rationalism of British classical economics. He, too, claimed that Schmoller was more of an historian than an economic theorist.

In 1940, after the outbreak of World War II, Walter Eucken wrote a blistering attack on Schmoller's legacy to German economics. He cited two factors which required improvements, the first of which was Schmoller's faulty concept of historical and social process as a continual evolution. He was, said Eucken, a veritable captive of the idea of progress. Eucken cited Thucydides's description of the horrors of the Civil War in 427 B. C., the excesses of the French Revolution at the end of the 18th century, and the horrors of the Bolshevik Revolution in 1917.[113] The second erroneous factor, according to Eucken, was Schmoller's inability to do economic theory; that is, he did not know or did not want to use the device of isolating economic phenomena from the rest of society. Hence, in Eucken's mind, the German Historical School was a step backwards, not a thrust forward, in the evolution of economics.[114]

From a perspective of almost fifty years, it seems that Eucken's attack on Schmoller had little to do whith Schmoller's actual legacy to economists. Eucken was a member of the Resistance Movement to Hitler's regime, with it's own political and economic program, and Eucken's famous *Antinomie* of economic orders was a sophisticated way to vent his frustrations against the Nazi regime. Actually Schmoller and Eucken shared the idea that one did not need a violent, Bolshevik-style revolution to improve the lot of the working masses. Schmoller strove to do it with legislation, Eucken with his "soziale Marktwirtschaft."

It was Joseph A. Schumpeter, who dealt with Schmoller's attitude towards this matter. He noted that "Schmoller always protested against an 'isolating' analysis of economic phenomena—he and his followers spoke of a 'method of isolation'—and held that their essence is lost when they are isolated. This view, of course, was simply the consequence of this resolve to feed economics exclusively on historical monographs."[115] Schumpeter went on to say that "in principle, if not quite in practice, the Schmollerian economist was in fact a *historically minded sociologist* in the latter term's widest meaning."[116] By the time Schmoller had published his *Grundriss*, Schumpeter noted, "he had silently unlearned the lessons of extreme 'historicism.'"[117] Schmoller theorized weakly, in Schumpeter's judgment. Yet in 1926, Schumpeter was still quite infatuated with Schmoller's work and his method.[118]

---

[113] "Wissenschaft im Stile Schmollers," in *Weltwirtschaftliches Archiv*, vol. 52, 1940, p. 475, p. 477, and p. 489.

[114] *Ibid.*, p. 495.

[115] Schumpeter, J. A., *History of Economic Analysis*, New York, Oxford University Press, 1954, p. 812.

[116] *Loc.cit.*

[117] *Ibid.*, p. 813.

In 1969, Schumpeter's star student, Erich Schneider, observed that shortly before the outbreak of World War I theoretical economics virtually did not exist in Germany.[119] Economists, educated in Schmollers's method, had the tendency to look back, not forward. Moritz J. Bonn, once president of the Business School of Berlin, wrote:

> The historians on whose preserves he [Schmoller] had poached called him a first-rate economist, while those economists who understood the complicated mechanism of modern economy praised him as a historian. Both were wrong. He was a first-rate sociologist who might be classified as an institutionalist, and a very brilliant essayist. He was learned and scholarly, yet his great work, *Principles of Economics,* reads like a clever travelogue on the social sciences— full of bright observations and of dissolving views. For he was a superrelativist whose answer was never "yes" or "no". He taught his pupils to look upon all economic problems as fluid, not to say slippery phenomena, the true inner meaning of which one could not grasp. This being the case, the right approach was to study history; if one were both courageous and inquisitive, one might describe but never appraise actual conditions. As to economic policies, it was wise to be cautious and to leave them to those who were in power; when they had made their decisions, one might provide them with facts and good reasons to justify their actions.[120]

Obviously the above account is not flattering to Schmoller: Bonn minced no words and showed considerable disrespect for Schmoller's monographs, his *Grundriss* and his legacy for the early welfare legislation of Germany. Bonn was a multi-lingual, high class journalist at best, who as a non-mathematical economist forever yearned for classroom certainties and fixities. Like Salin, he made a reputation in debunking Schmoller. Yet in restrospect, Schmoller, the father of the modern welfare state, with all his faults, relativism, errors, unfortunate and gratuitous epithets about people, adversaries, and different nationalities, produced a work that is still a source book, a veritable goldmine.

We are celebrating the sesquicentennial of his birth in 1988. The Federal Republic of Germany is the envy of postwar Western Europe. The German Democratic Republic is not quite the material paragon of the socialist countries of Eastern Europe, but it has evolved into a considerable welfare state.

Schmoller was already concerned about the material welfare of the industrial masses some 125 years ago. Even then, he pleaded for the market-based economy and the retention of the private property of the means of production. His opponents, the Marxists and all the nihilists of that time, wanted to destroy the existing order, expropriate the property of the rich, and then await results.

---

[118] Schumpeter, J., "Gustav v. Schmoller und die Probleme von heute," *Schmollers Jahrbuch,* vol. 50, 1926, pp. 2-3.

[119] Schneider, E., "Rückblick auf ein halbes Jahrhundert der Wirtschaftswissenschaft, (1918-1968)" in *Weltwirtschaftliches Archiv,* vol. 102, 1969, p. 157.

[120] Bonn, M. J., *Wandering Scholar,* New York, The John Day Company, 1948, p. 50.

Schmoller was not a classroom economist, seeking eternal verities. He knew that he was place- and time-bound. He wanted to save German masses from a violent, Communist-led revolution. He feared the Marxists and he was not popular with the fashionable crowd of "progressive" leanings. As late as 1983, the pronouncement on Schmoller in America was that his methods "were not fit to cope with theoretical problems."[121] As emphasized repeatedly, Schmoller's concern was how to cope with the "social fiasco" of the laissez-faire system.[122] His concerns were the pressing social problems of the day, not speculative hypotheses, or equations and matrices on the blackboard.

Regardless of what has been the fate of Schmoller's *Grundriss* over time, it may be proper to conclude this section by citing a translated passage from Schmoller's own preface to *Grundriss II*:

However incomplete my *Grundriss* may remain, however little it may satisfy the theoretical economist or the individual historian, the effort at a general synthesis is not superfluous and not unfruitful. It had to be undertaken by an economic historian, one who has always considered it a false charge against himself that he was striving for description, not for a general understanding of the laws of economic life. Only with such a representation created from the whole can one serve the greater purpose of all scientific understanding. I do not pride myself too much on my work when I say that I have written it in the service of the leading economic ideas and trends of our time and of the ideals which rule my life. Without coming too close to other fields, I believe I may say that it is clear that a *Grundriss* of economic theory has been written by a scholar who is as much an historian of constitutional, administrative, and economic life as an economist, who has followed the process of psychological, social as well as economic development and who, with the far greater means of present-day economic history, has attacked the work which Roscher began fifty years ago.[123]

In short, Schmoller's *Grundriss* reflected his lifelong concern with the social consequences of rapid industrialization of Germany and with what could be done to integrate the industrial workers into the mainstream of German society by way of social legislation. He also aimed to collect social statistics so as to acquire firm ground under his feet, very similar to Wassily Leontief's present-day quest to collect firm data for the technology matrices in his Input-Output system.[124] In addition, he made many detailed historical studies, with particular

---

[121] Pribram, K., *A History of Economic Reasoning*, Baltimore, The Johns Hopkins University Press, 1983, p. 218.

[122] Schmoller, G., *Die soziale Frage. Klassenbildung, Arbeiterfrage, Klassenkampf*, München, Duncker & Humblot, 1918, p. 394.

[123] Anderson, P. R., *op.cit.*, p. 301.

[124] Leontief, W., "Why Economics Needs Input-Output Analysis," in *Challenge*, vol. 28, # 1, 1985, p. 29.

interest in public administration. The proper education of the German government officials was of utmost importance for him.

Schmoller's third concern was of a methodological nature. Unlike the British classical economists, as well as today's mathematical economic theorists, who always dealt with the laws and explanations of "what is" and who were proud to maintain their *Wertfreiheit*, Schmoller disliked the "laissez-faire" capitalist system and had firmly rejected the *Wertfreiheit* postulate. In fact, he was quite an Anglophobe. He detested the fashionable Marxist literature and particularly the Marxist vision of the "new" socialist social order. With this in mind, Schmoller was thinking in terms of different social orders. Marxist "central despotism" to him meant a society with no privately-owned means of production, absence of a market economy, and a totalitarian political structure. He did not want any of that, and he forever preached his "ought to be's." Schmoller cast his "ought to be's" in terms of a market economy, presence of private and corporate ownership of the means of production, a political system of plurality. He also circumscribed civil rights, but did approve of the multi-party parliamentary system.[125] He was harshly castigated for his *normative values*, particularly during the *Werturteilstreit* of 1909 by Max Weber and Werner Sombart. It is interesting and ironic, almost 80 years after the event and in view of the experiences of the Soviet Union during the 1930's, that most of the Russian mathematical economists—who maintained their value-free stance— disappeared in Stalin's purges. They were competent scholars but *apolitical*, committed to *Wertfreiheit*, and that may have been the reason for their disappearance in Stalin's bloodbath.[126]

It is this kind of experience that Schmoller probably wanted to prevent at all cost for his Germany. It is for this reason that he used the *Verein für Socialpolitik* to prepare the necessary social and welfare legislation, successfully cultivated men in authority, and was influential in gaining support of these men to pass legislation, designed to overcome the vicious class antagonisms between the property-owning class and the industrial workers. In Schumpeter's view, Schmoller was remarkably successful on this score.[127]

---

[125] Schön, M., "Gustav Schmoller and Max Weber," in *Max Weber and His Contemporaries*, London, Allen & Unwin, 1987, p. 66.

[126] No one knows exactly the number of Stalin's victims. Medvedev, in his *Let History Judge*, 1971, p. 239 estimated that the 1930's four to five million people were arrested. Robert Conquest, in his *The Great Terror: Stalin's Purge of the Thirties*, 1968, p. 532, mentioned nine million people in captivity at the end of 1938. Still another source claimed that the "total number in the labor and concentration camps [was] estimated to be between 15 and 20 million"; see, Byckowski, G., "Joseph V. Stalin: Paranoia and the Dictatorship of the Proletariat," in *The Psychoanalytic Interpretation of History*, edited by B. S. Wolman, New York, Basic Books, 1971, p. 130. In the summer of 1987, a source from Moscow claimed that 17 million people perished during Stalin's years of terror.

[127] Schumpeter, J., "Gustav v. Schmoller und die Probleme von Heute," in *Schmollers Jahrbuch*, 50, 1926, p. 3.

Alas, today Schmoller is almost always dismissed in America as a member of the younger German Historical School of Economics. No self-respecting authors on economic thought deal with him and his work, except in passing— maybe in a footnote. Very few contemporary economists think in terms of a social order these days, except those specializing in comparative systems. The mainstream economists dismiss those as marginal economists. Furthermore, no self-respecting economist will be interested in soiling his hands and getting involved with the preparation of material for social legislation, such as the current overhaul of America's welfare system. Finally, economists adhere strictly to the value-free stance and claim to be *apolitical* in their work.

And, of course, it was the mathematical revolution of the post-world War II period that swept Schmoller out of mainstream economics all over the world. Today economists at the American Ivy-League universities as a rule hold the Bachelor of Science degree in mathematics or physics, the M.S. in statistics or computer science, and the Ph.D. in econometrics. Mathematical shorthand has almost replaced spoken and written English. Economists of such education and training have a tendency to relegate the social, demographic, attitudinal, political, and institutional factors to the *ceteris paribus* cage. Put differently, the economic theorists of today have acquired an irresistible predilection for deductive reasoning.

Yet many other economists do not like this trend. One is Professor Wassily Leontief of New York University, a Nobel Laureate in Economics for 1973. In 1982, he wrote that the present-day professional journals of economics "are filled with mathematical formulas leading the reader from sets of more or less plausible but entirely arbitrary assumptions to precisely stated but irrelevant theoretical conclusions."[128] In short, overvaluation of mathematical economics has led to policy-irrelevancy and bitter denunciation of academic economics in contemporary America.[129]

Professor Alfred S. Eichner of Rutgers University has even charged that present-day economics has become a "closed system of ideas," like a religion.[130] And, finally, at the end of 1985, Professor Charles P. Kindleberger of MIT charged that "economists are very good at *a priori* reasoning but do not want their models 'tarnished with the realities of a peculiar institutional structure' in the belief that reality would make the models 'inferior from a methodological perspective.'"[131]

---

[128] Leontief, W., "Academic Economics," in *Science*, vol. 217, 1982, p. 104.

[129] Bell, D. and I. Kristol (eds.), *The Crisis in Economic Theory*, New York, Basic Books, 1981, pp. 201-218.

[130] Eichner, A. S., *Why Economics is Not Yet a Science*, Armonk, N.Y., M. E. Sharpe, 1983, Preface, p. XIII and pp. 3-14.

[131] Silk, L., "Lost Standing of Economists," in *The New York Times*, January 3, 1986, D-2. See also, C. P. Kindleberger, "International Public Goods without International Government," in *American Economic Review*, vol. 76, # 1, March, 1986, pp. 1-11.

6*

Yet the change was inevitable, and economists, particularly those with open minds, ears and eyes, slowly and imperceptibly pushed for widening the scope of economic inquiry. For example, Nicholas Georgescu-Roegen, popularized the notion of bioeconomics. He wrote in one of his publications that the term economics "is intended to make us bear in mind continuously the biological origin of the economic process and to spotlight the problem of mankind's existence with a limited store of accessible resources, unevenly located and unequally appropriated."[132]

Professors Kenneth Boulding, Herman Daley, Edward O. Wilson, Konrad Lorenz, and Rupert Riedl have stressed in their writings over the last two decades that economists cannot afford to overlook forever the biological foundations of economic activity. These are the very dimensions of social evolution which Schmoller discussed at considerable length in his *first* volume of the *Grundriss* in the Introduction, second section, in nine subsections, pp. 6-75. Yet it was precisely this part that was considered useless for economists.

Economists today are aware of the fact that the human species, as members of the animal kingdom, live as other species do, by taking low entropy from the natural environment and discharging it back into that environment as high entropy waste. The bioeconomists interpret past and present economic systems as a subset of larger processes taking place in the world. This rising school of new economics is based upon the holistic view of nature, man, and society, and it rejects the reductionist and isolationist methods of modern economics, including those of the economic theorists. The work by Konrad Lorenz[133] and Rupert Riedl[134] comes readily to mind. Professor Leopold Kohr has called the economists' attention to the economic and social problems emanating from the concept of size. His pathbreaking work, *The Breakdown of Nations*, was published in 1957. The book on the diseconomies of scale was published in 1977 as *The Overdeveloped Nations*. E. F. Schumacher merely popularized Kohr's message with his book, *Small is Beautiful*. Kenneth Boulding, the former economic theorist, has for almost two decades argued that evolution, a holistic approach because of the biological base of society cannot be "isolated away" by economists.[135]

American Institutionalists, or rather Neo-Institutionalists are pleading for greater use of neighboring fields, surrounding economics, and avoidance of the exclusive reliance on willfull mathematical speculation and modeling. This

[132] Georgescu-Roegen, N., "Inequality, Limits and Growth from a Bioeconomic Viewpoint," in *Review of Social Economy*, vol. 35, # 3, 1977, pp. 361-75.

[133] Lorenz, K., *On Agression* and *Behind the Mirror. A Search for a Natural History of Human Knowledge*, New York, A Harvest/HBJ Book, 1978.

[134] Riedl, R., *Kultur-Spätzündung der Evolution? Antworten auf Fragen an die Evolutions- und Erkenntnistheorie*, Munich, Piper, 1987, especially pp. 111-191, dealing with nature and society.

[135] Boulding, K., *Evolutionary Economics*, Beverly Hills, Ca., Sage Publications, 1981.

American heteredox neoinstitutionalism has numerous intellectual and methodological linkages to Schmoller.[136] Furthermore, G. L. S. Shackle, the sage of contemporary English economists, wrote in 1983 that the economics profession of today needs "to make case studies, rather than allegedly 'general' theories, the vehicle of our thought."[137] And, finally, the economics profession in America is taking steps to counter the excessive mathematization of the profession. In the summer of 1987, the American Economic Association launched a new journal, called *The Journal of Economic Perspectives,* designed "to fill a gap between the general interest press and existing academic economics journals."[138] The new journal will serve as a scholarly economics journal for the general audience of economists. Another journal, *Forum,* was also launched, and is devoted to a thorough, practical discussion of policies relating to energy, economic development, and the environment. A couple of years ago, *Economics and Philosophy,* a semi-annual journal made its appearance to serve as bridge between the increasingly artificial disciplinary boundaries that divide them. It also called to the attention of the economists that their work in both positive and normative economics depends on methodological and ethical commitments which require philosophical study. The message is slowly emerging that economics or political economy cannot be reduced to speculative quantification without hard data. Maybe Schmoller deliberately disparaged economic theory, so as to acquire a firmer ground under his feet. Alas, the mathematical revolution of economics swept away whatever firm ground economists had had under their feet. It also jettisoned as excess baggage all the neighboring fields which encase economics. An economist who knows nothing but economics, needs help, John Stuart Mill (1806-1873) said more than a century ago. It may be that Schmoller's *Grundriss,* in the original or in the eventual English-translation, could be of some help.

[136] Langlois, R. N., editor, *Economics as a Process. Essays in the New Institutional Economics,* New York, Cambridge University Press, 1986.

[137] Shackle, G. L. S., review of *The Politics and Philosophy of Economics,* by T. W. Hutchinson, Oxford, Blackwell, 1981, in *The Economic Journal,* vol. 93, March, 1983, p. 224.

[138] "Foreword", vol. 1, #1, 1987, p. 3. See also, Herron, C. R., "Economist to Economist, in English," *The New York Times,* September 27, 1987.

Chapter VI

The Impact of Gustav Schmoller's Work on American Economics

Before approaching the question of the impact and eventual legacy of Schmoller on the American intellectual scene, it is useful to recall a few salient developments of the second half of the 19th century. The end of the bloody and protracted American Civil War came in 1865. The industrial North ground into dust the agricultural Confederacy of the Southern States. Its end encouraged political and economic centralization of America. Washington, D.C. sparkled as the administrative, legislative, and judicial center of the United States.

In 1871, Europe witnessed the emergence of the unified German Reich. For centuries, Germany had been merely a geographic concept, consisting of some 300 German-speaking kingdoms, duchies, and free cities. After the end of the Napoleonic wars in 1815, their number was reduced to 38. Of these states, Prussia was marked by a unique pattern of evolution. From a small, inconsequential kingdom, it grew into a European power, after coming dangerously close to extinction, like its eastern neighbor Poland. The Seven Year War (1756-1763) nearly brought about the demise of Prussia, which, at that time, was ruled by Frederick the Great (1712-1786).[1] Frederick managed to antagonize his neighbors and eventually found himself encircled by an alliance of France, Austria, Russia, and Sweden. Prussia survived in the end—barely— because of two fortunate turns of events: its ally, Great Britain, was victorious in its overseas (and high seas) confrontation with France; and its major enemy, Russia, was taken out of the Seven Year War after the death of Tsarina Elizabeth. Elizabeth, Peter's daughter and an old enemy of Prussia, was succeeded by her nephew, Peter III of Schleswig-Holstein, who was an ardent admirer of Frederick the Great. Peter III ordered the Russian army to withdraw from Prussia. Empress Maria Theresa of Austria, weary of the prolonged bloodshed, quit too. In any event, Prussia survived.

In the early 19th century, Napoleon's armies rode roughshod over the entire European continent. Napoleon made and un-made kings; exacted reparations from defeated kingdoms, dukedoms, and cities; promulgated new laws; and introduced the new spirit of liberty, fraternity, and equality into French-occupied Europe. Eventually, Napoleon's armies were destroyed in Russia in

---

[1] Mitford, N., *Frederick the Great,* New York, Harper and Row, 1970, pp. 133-149.

1812, and he suffered his ultimate defeat in mid-1815 at Waterloo. Thus, Prussia survived again.

From 1815 to 1848, Europe was dominated by the Tripartite Alliance of Russia, Prussia, and Austria, which had been created by Metternich, Austria's well-known foreign minister, during the Vienna conference of 1815.[2] By 1848, however, Europe, particularly Germany and France and the Low Countries, was virtually torn asunder by rising demands for written constitutions, civil rights, and the elimination of the divine rights for ruling royal dynasties. Rapid industrialization, and the rising middle classes of merchants, industrialists, and exporters combined with the swelling numbers of property-less industrial workers, known as proletarians, to cause social change. The *Communist Manifesto* of 1848 inspired millions of proletarians to embrace socialism, the new creed for material betterment in this world rather than in the next. This social agitation led to a wave of repression and attempts to slow down the ascendancy of the new social classes. By the mid-1850's, rabid nationalism was the new mode of politics and diplomacy on the European continent.

The defeat of France in the short Franco-Prussian war of 1871 led to the emergence of a united Germany. The Second German Reich, now a reality under Kaiser Wilhelm I, sought equality with England and Russia. In time, these great empires felt threatened by this parvenu.

In the 19th century, Prussia and the other German states underwent rapid industrialization. Railroad building and the growth of the iron-making and iron-working, chemical, and machine-building industries changed the landscape profoundly. The inevitable decline of the rural population, the swelling numbers of the urban population, the spreading materialism and greater egalitarianism, and the emergence of a superb system of higher education and empirical research, well-funded and directed from Berlin, became magic to many foreigners, including Americans. They flocked to Germany in great numbers after the unification of the German Reich. The future engineers, chemists, and physicists were attracted by its excellent research institutes and famous academics. The future economists were drawn to Germany by the writings of Wilhelm Roscher, Bruno Hildebrand, and Karl Knies, who proposed new and almost radical departures in economic thought. These economists were the great innovators of the day in their profession. At that time, the broad-based German economists were doing empirical work of considerable merit, even from the contemporary perspective.[3]

As reported by Professor Joseph Dorfman in 1955, the professional science of economics did not exist in the United States before the 1880s or even 1890s. Prior

---

[2] Maehl, W. H., *Germany in Western Civilization,* University of Alabama, The University of Alabama Press, 1981, pp. 306-320.

[3] Obershall, A., *Empirical Social Research in Germany, 1848-1914,* The Hague, Mouton and Company, 1965, see the Preface and pp. 76-92.

to that time, economics, as a rule, was taught in the philosophy or social science department.[4] In fact, during the first one hundred years of America's existence, economics as an independent discipline was a rather wilted flower. In an essay written in America's centennial year, Charles F. Dunbar said Americans had contributed virtually nothing to the development of economic theory.[5] Furthermore, before the Civil War, there was no need for professional economists for two reasons. First, the major economic and social issues were left to state legislatures to be either solved or not resolved by politicians who knew nothing about economics and did not care to know. Second, making money was magic to the ambitious and intelligent young men, and, for this reason, it was difficult to attract able minds to social sciences in general and to economics in particular.[6]

And yet, even before the Civil War, America could boast of such distinguished historians as Prescott and Bancroft. And how can one ever forget the flowering of American literature, represented by such men as Cooper, Irving, Poe, Longfellow, Hawthorne, and Emerson? In other words, prior to the Civil War, America was by no means a nation of 'dollar chasers,' as Farnam, the German-educated economist, once put it.

What were some of the reasons for the relative underdevelopment of economics during that period? The answers lay, in part, in the legal framework of the United States. America's federal and state constitutions attempted to codify the general framework of government activity as well as certain civil liberties of its citizens. These constitutions imposed certain restrictions upon the federal government and certain obligations on the states. To maintain peaceful relations between the federal government and the various states, the interpretation of the state constitutions and of the Constitution itself was turned over to the country's courts. This unique feature of the American system of government had certain distinct disadvantages for the evolution of the economics profession because every economic question could potentially be turned into a legal question and every piece of legislation could be declared unconstitutional by the Supreme court.[7]

---

[4] Dorfman, J., "The Role of the German Historical School in American Economic Thought," in *American Economic Review,* vol. 45, # 2, 1955, p. 31.

[5] Dunbar, C. F., "Economic Science in America," *The North American Review,* vol. 122, 1876, pp. 124-154.

[6] Farnam, H. W., "Deutsch-amerikanische Beziehungen in der Volkswirtschaftslehre," in *Die Entwicklung der deutschen Volkswirtschaftslehre im neunzehnten Jahrhundert. Gustav Schmoller zur siebzigsten Wiederkehr seines Geburtstages 24. Juni 1908,* vol. I, Leipzig, Duncker and Humblot, 1908, p. 3.

[7] Peltason, J. W., *Understanding the Constitution,* Tenth Edition, New York, Holt, Rinehart and Winston, 1985, chapter on the "Basic Features of the Constitution," pp. 17-35. See also, Tocqueville, A. de, *Democracy in America,* vol. I, chapter VI called "Judicial Power in the United States, and Its Influence on Political Society," New York, Vintage Books, 1945, pp. 102-109.

Another reason for the relative backwardness of the economics profession prior to 1861 was the fact that the great majority of the population was engaged in farming and the urban population constituted about 20 percent of the total population. Also, as Farnam writes, the prevailing public opinion of the country held that "every decent human being could occupy almost any government office of the land."[8] The widely-accepted "spoils system" of government appointments meant that there was no sustained demand for well-trained and educated government officials by federal, state, or local government. Furthermore, there prevailed a certain disdain and almost contempt by the practical businessman, the proverbial American "Mr. Babbit", for the poorly paid university professors or scientists. Only the "dumb" ones taught; all bright folks made money. Finally, the relative poverty of American universities of the time meant that economic subjects were usually taught together with philosophy by the president of a university, who, as a rule, was a successful businessmen himself. He had little time to specialize in any aspect of economics and had no incentive to write books or deliver papers at conferences. He was busy making money. His mind was geared to solving pressing economic problems of the day and making money in the process and he did not wish to waste time on "armchair economics."

The first American economist of considerable standing was Benjamin Franklin (1706-1790), but the man who unquestionably put American economics on the map was Alexander Hamilton (1756-1804), the first Secretary of the Treasury. Hamilton's *Report on Manufacturers*, submitted to Congress on December 5, 1791, in one of the "great American state papers and in a sense may be the first American treatise on political economy."[9] Having surveyed the status of industry in the newly-founded nation and having given thought to its industrial future, economic progress, and well-being, Hamilton proceeded to reject the laissez-faire wisdom of Adam Smith for the recently-sovereign United States of America. Instead, his idea of nurturing "infant industries" by protecting them through tariffs eventually found eager ears in this country and was "repeated for a century and a half after he put them forward."[10]

What Adam Smith preached in the form of the powerful doctrine of individualism, self-incentive, and private profit, Hamilton qualified and partly rejected. Smith called his idea universal and absolute, applicable to all places and valid at all times. Hamilton disagreed. What may have been true for England in

---

[8] Farnam, H. W., *op.cit.*, p. 4.

[9] Mitchell, Broadus and Louise P., *American Economic History*, Boston, Houghton Mifflin Company, 1947, p. 263.

[10] Mitchell, B., *Alexander Hamilton. A Concise Biography*, New York, Oxford University Press, 1976, p. 217. See also, Mitchell, B., "Alexander Hamilton, Executive Power and the New Nation," in *Presidential Studies Quarterly*, vol. 17, # 2, 1987, p. 342. For a fuller treatment of the subject, see Mitchell, B., *Alexander Hamilton, 1788-1804*, New York, The Macmillan Company, 1962, chapter 8 called 'Stimulants to Manufacture,' pp. 138-153.

1776 was not necessarily valid, applicable, and transplantable to the United States around 1800. Hamilton simply rejected Smith's scenario; he did not like his dictum of benevolence of laissez-faire. On the contrary, he advocated the use of selective government stimulation and encouragement in establishing manufacturing industries in the new country. He knew from experience what awesome competitive pressures the British merchants could bring to bear. Without protection, the new American industries stood no chance. Hamilton also knew that the British mercantile interests were ably supported by the British navy.

Another American, not an economist by training but a relatively idle lawyer of Baltimore, Daniel Raymond, published in 1820 his *Thoughts on Political Economy*.[11] Raymond was a sharp critic of the excessive laissez-faire doctrine and had no use for the natural laws of social harmony and for free trade. As an American, a citizen of a sovereign but undeveloped and agricultural country, he argued that the aim of political economy should be the promulgation of rules, laws, and regulations which maximized the well-being of American citizens. He energetically advocated the use of protective tariffs to aid in industrializing America.

Even though Raymond's book never had much influence on the academic economists, it probably had considerable influence on the relations between American and German economists. It is entirely possible, for example, that Friedrich List was influenced by Raymond's work. In fact, at the end of the 19th century, Charles P. Neill, in his essay on Raymond, tried to indicate the close parallels between List's basic ideas and a new 1823 work by Raymond.[12] In Farnam's view, it was Friedrich List who made the first contacts between American and German economists.[13] In any event, Hamilton's suggestions of government-aided measures for the industrialization of agricultural America were further elaborated by Friedrich List, a German immigrant residing in Pennsylvania, and by Henry C. Carey, of Philadelphia, Pennsylvania. These two writers contradicted Adam Smith's dictum that private enterprise, self-interest, competition, and division of labor were applicable everywhere in the world. Nations are in different stages of development, the Americans argued, and for this reason required different policy measures. Laissez-faire might have suited Britain in the late 18th century, but "let alone" economic policies were useless for the United States and for Germany. To catch up with Britain, Hamilton, List, Raymond, and Carey called for positive encouragement by government authorities. An industry must be protected in order to be established. In short, the Americans said Adam Smith's principles of political economy were not of universal applicability but were relative to time and place.

---

[11] Petrella, F.,"Daniel Raymond, Adam Smith, and Classical Growth Theory: An Inquiry into the Nature and Causes of the Wealth of America," in *History of Political Economy*, vol. 19, # 2, 1987, pp. 239-259.

[12] Neill, C. P., *Daniel Raymond*, Baltimore, 1897, Johns Hopkins Studies, Series 15, # 6.

[13] Farnam, H. W., *op.cit.*, p. 6.

List had settled near Tamaqua, on the banks of the Little Schuykill River in Pennsylvania, where he opened a coal mine, operated a railway and prospered.[14] He was very busy between 1827 and 1839, when he edited the German language newspaper, the *Readinger Adler*. While there, he got involved in a controversy over the merits of the so- called "American System" of stimulating industrial growth through high tariffs and programs of federally financed public works. List emerged a well-known man from this controversy.In 1827, the protectionists of Pennsylvania mounted a vigorous campaign to safeguard the "infant industries." It was this campaign and the consequent debates that eventually led to List's major work, *The National System of Political Economy*. The free-traders were appalled by what List preached, considering it pure economic heresy. The work, which was published in 1841, focused on *the nation*, not on the private profit-seeking businessman. The creation of value by increasing specialization and division of labor was of less importance to List than was the national capacity to produce goods and services. The power and the capacity to produce wealth were more important than wealth itself.

List was probably one of the first people in the first third of the 19th century to abandon laissez-faire and the natural law of British political economists. He decried "let alone" individualism and the virtual "do-nothing" government of Adam Smith and promoted the power of government in an organized community. Like Alexander Hamilton before him, he pleaded for guidance and correction by government. He did not preach Marxian socialism, anarchism, or communism. He was a staunch advocate of private ownership of the means of production and he cherished the democratic system of individual liberty. He also extolled the virtues of coordination and efficiency in the market economy. He stressed, however, that British political economists paid no attention to the concept of the *nation*, and he warned his readers—politicians and government officials—that a nation could have interests and purposes different from those of individuals. All this was heresy to the die-hard practitioners of classical economics.

List eventually returned to Germany and died there in 1846. But his influence on America, American tariff policy, and on American economists has been lasting, even if today it has been forgotten by academics. List was, obviously, the first vital and lasting link between German and American economists.

Around the middle of the 19th century, Henry C. Carey, too, helped develop intellectual contacts between the two countries. Carey had not studied in Germany, but he had visited the country, liked it, and developed an enormous respect for things German. In his *Principles of Social Science* he wrote that "Germany stands first in Europe in point of intellectual development and in advancing the physical and moral condition of the people with a rapidity

---

[14] Henderson, W. O., *Friedrich List. Economist and Visionary, 1789-1846*, London, Frank Cass, 1983, pp. 68-72. See also, Lenz, F., *Friedrich List und die deutsche Einheit*, (1789-1846), Stuttgart, Deutsche Verlagsanstalt, 1946, pp. 105-114.

exceeding that of any other portion of the eastern hemisphere."[15] In spite of
these sporadic contacts, Farnam concluded that prior to the outbreak of the
Civil War in 1861, it was hardly possible to talk about the existence of an
American Political Economy. In his mind, none existed.[16] After the end of the
Civil War, the industrialization of America accelerated. Yet many Americans
had seen and had not forgotten the social ills of the English factory towns. And
the works of Charles Dickens and other well-known English literary giants of
the time, which decried the social horrors of industrialization under the auspices
of laissez-faire, were widely read in America. Furthermore, utopian colonies
were set up in many parts of the United States in the hope of avoiding the
unintended social consequences of England's rapid industrialization. Robert
Owen's 'New Harmony' in Indiana was probably the best known.

Economists, social scientists, religious leaders, journalists, and even politicians questioned the adequacy of the classical school of economics and its ability
to cope with the numerous social and human problems of rapid industrialization
under the conditions of unfettered 'laissez-faire.'

It was in this atmosphere that the German departure in economic thought,
made by such men as Roscher, Hildebrand, Knies, Cohn, Schmoller, Brentano,
and Wagner, made a great impression on young Americans.[17] The German
economists had provided a rationale for combatting the arrogant individualism
of the time, and the young Yanks adopted their teachings with enthusiasm.[18]

In the 19th century, well-to-do young Americans were sent on the "Grand
Tour of Europe" to round out their classical education. Such tours usually
started in Great Britain and continued through Germany and France and on to
Italy and Greece. Some even went to the Holy Land. (American know well the
pleasures and pains of such tours as described by Mark Twain in his *The Innocents
Abroad, or, the New Pilgrim's Progress,* published in 1869). Because graduate
schools hardly existed in America until the late 19th century, young Americans
wanting to complete their professional education had to look abroad. They were
particularly drawn to Germany because of the quality and reputation of its
magnificent universities. These Americans were serious students, not academic
dilettanti.[19] They were generally of two types: future scientists, primarily
chemists, such as Caldwell, Chandler, and Nicholas; and men of letters, such as
Bancroft, Everett, and Longfellow. English universities at that time had the
reputation of being outdated. Furthermore, Cambridge and Oxford still

---

[15] 1867 edition, vol. 2, p. 146, quoted by Farnam, H. W., *op.cit.,* pp. 6-7.

[16] Farnam, H. W., *op.cit.,* p. 7.

[17] Dorfman, J., "The Role of the German Historical School in American Economic
Thought," in *American Economic Review,* vol. 45, 1955, p. 17.

[18] *Ibid.,* p. 28.

[19] Buchloh, P. G. and Rix, W. T., *American Colony of Göttingen. Historical and Other
Data collected between the Years 1855 and 1888,* Göttingen, Vandenhoeck and Ruprecht,
1976, p. 11.

"required students to acknowledge the thirty-nine articles of the Anglican Church ... This was anathema to the American young men and went against the grain of other non-Anglican Protestants."[20] In contrast, German universities had been revamped along the lines suggested by the Humboldtian educational reforms in the early 19th century. They had transformed science "into a status approaching that of a professional career and into a bureaucratic, organized activity."[21] This transformation made research a necessary qualification for a university career, and an indispensable function of a university professor. For all these reasons, an estimated 9000 Americans went to Germany to study[22] between 1820 and 1920. The University of Göttingen, [since 1866] one of the most dynamic of Prussian universitites, was particularly attractive to Americans.

In the 18th century German university, a great deal of clerical supervision was the norm. It was only after the establishment of the University of Berlin in 1809 that a veritable revolution swept through the German universities. The changes were quite rapid, because science and scientific progress in Germany had to be accomodated and cultivated in an "inimical envrionment" where there was neither freedom of speech nor social equality.[23] Eventually, the initial obstacles were overcome and, by the mid-1850s, it could be said that "the peculiar character of the German universities lies in the fact that it closely connects research and teaching."[24] Futhermore, *Lehrfreiheit* and *Lernfreiheit* were the two fundamental principles of the German universities. *Lehrfreiheit* refers to the freedom of teaching what the academic believes in, and the conviction that the subject-matter of his teaching "must not be prescribed for him."[25] Today this term is usually translated into academic freedom.

Lernfreiheit, freedom for the student, is the corollary of freedom for the university professor. It assumes that the professor is an independent scholar[26] who will teach the student how to acquire independence of thought in his field of specialization. At the end of the 19th century, *Lehrfreiheit* and *Lernfreiheit* were "as good as unlimited."[27]

The overall impact of such restructured German universities was that "some German universities became the center and sometimes virtually the seats of world-wide scientific communities in their respective fields."[28] By sheer con-

---

[20] *Ibid.*, p. 14.

[21] Ben-David, J., *The Scientist's Role in Society*, Englewood Cliffs, New Jersey, Prentice-Hall, 1971, p. 108.

[22] Herbst, J., *op.cit.*, pp. 1-2.

[23] Ben-David J., *ibid.*, p. 119.

[24] Paulsen, F., *The German Universities. Their Character and Historic Development*, New York, Macmillan, 1895, p. XXI.

[25] Paulsen, F., *ibid.*, p. 161.

[26] Paulsen, F., *ibid.*, p. 201.

[27] *Loc.cit.*

[28] Ben-David, J., *op.cit.*, p. 124.

centration of efforts, German scientists had an edge over everyone else in the world. Mindful of that edge, American youngsters flocked in thousands to the Universities of Berlin, Heidelberg, Göttingen, and Leipzig. In addition to becoming the world's leader in the various fields of natural sciences and mathematics, German universities also gained prominence in social sciences, such as sociology, history, economics, and experimental psychology. This German-led development was discussed in Chapter Two and is of particular relevance here. German economists, like Wilhelm Roscher, Bruno Hildebrand, Karl Knies, Gustav Schmoller, Adolph Wagner, Lujo Brentano, have popularly — and in this writer's mind mistakenly — been dubbed members of the German Historical School of Economics. To this writer, these economists could have been more aptly called Welfare-oriented economists or, following the suggestion by Johannes Conrad, advocates of policy-making economics.[29] These German economists were bent on preventing the Marxist-inspired socialists from revamping Germany with Marxist ideology, dictatorship of the proletariat, elimination of the private ownership of the means of production in agriculture and industry, and elimination of the market economy. This new German school of economics was concerned with "what not ought to be" in Germany and, for this reason, they were dubbed the "socialists of the chair," the "academic socialists," "sugar-water socialists," the "saliva-lickers of the bourgeoisie," or simply "not-authentic socialists" by Marxists and Laissez-Fairists. These economists strove to avoid the social fiasco of laissez-fairist England of the first half of the 19th century. With this in mind, in 1872, they formed the *Verein für Socialpolitik*, designed to mitigate the unrestricted interaction of unequal private interests in the market place. To them common welfare was more important than the narrow private interests. The members of the *Verein* were united in their opposition, on moral grounds, to the natural-law doctrines of classical economics, and they all believed that governments must protect the economically weak from the economically strong and greedy by promulgating indispensable welfare legislation.[30] These German academic socialists condemned the actions of anarchists, terrorists, and bomb-throwing nihilists. The *Verein* members also stressed "the indispensability of historical study for the development of legislation," designed to improve the social and material lot of the industrial masses of Germany.[31]

Once the trickle of young Americans going to German universities became a stream, a unique and today almost forgotten transfer of culture got under way. From Germany to America in relentless flows streamed machinery, technology,

---

[29] Conrad, J., *Grundriss zum Studium der politischen Oekonomie*, Erster Teil, 11th edition, Jena, Verlag von Gustav Fischer, 1923, p. 509. See also, Diehl, K., "Johannes Conrad," in *Jahrbücher für Nationalökonomie und Statistik*, vol. 104, 1915, pp. 737 and 753, where one finds the names of Conrad's American students of economics.

[30] Herbst, J., *op.cit.*, pp. 144-45.

[31] *Ibid.*, p. 148.

inventions, scientific know-how, and German-trained American brainpower.[32] Many social scientists among these young men contributed substantially to the renaissance of America's intellectual life in the 1870s and 1880s.[33] The transfer of German culture continued up to the outbreak of World War I. It diminished rapidly in the 1920s, and with the onset of the Nazi persecution of the Jews, things German became viewed as barbaric. Most Americans today are virtually unaware of the half a century of intense intellectual links which existed between Germany and the United States prior to World War I.

Few quantitative data exist on the exact numbers of American economists who studied in Europe. In 1906, Professor Henry W. Farnam of Yale University sent out 126 questionnaires to former social science students in Europe; 116 replied. Of them, one-half had studied in Germany. According to this survey, John B. Clark was the first to go to Germany in 1873 after the Civil War. He remained there for two years and studied under Wilhelm Roscher and Karl Knies. Eventually, he became a professor at Columbia University. In 1875, he was followed by Henry W. Farnam, Edmund J. James (later President of the University of Illinois), and Joseph French Johnson, later a professor at New York University. In 1876, Simon N. Patten, later professor of economics at the University of Pennsylvania, and, in 1877, Richard T. Ely, who later taught at Johns Hopkins University and the University of Wisconsin followed suit. Arthur T. Hadley, later president of Yale University, went to Germany in 1877, Frank W. Taussig, later at Harvard University, went to Germany where he spent a winter semester at the University of Berlin, studying Roman law and political economy. Later on in life, Taussig often acknowledged the influence of Adolph Wagner.[34] Also in 1879, E. R. A. Seligman, later at Columbia University, and Albion W. Small, later professor of sociology at the University of Chicago, followed. Many others followed in the 1880s, even though their names are almost forgotten today.[35]

In 1890, Edwin R. Gay, later at Harvard University, went to Germany and stayed for more than a decade.[36] J. Laurence Laughlin, later of the University of Chicago, sailed for Germany in 1891 and Francis Walker went in 1892. Many, many others followed.[37] Approximately one third of all American social science

---

[32] See for instance, *The Greatest of Expositions Completely Illustrated*, St. Louis, 1904, p. 24, 64 and 84 for German exhibits.

[33] Commager, H. S., *The American Mind. An Interpretation of American Thought and Character. Since the 1880s*, New Haven, Yale University Press, 1950, pp.227-246 and pp. 310-335. See also, Dorfman, J., op.cit., p. 17.

[34] Schumpeter, J. A., *Ten Great Economists*, New York, Oxford University Press, 1951, p. 195.

[35] Dorfman, J., *The Economic Mind in American Civilization*, vol. 3, 1865-1918, New York, August M. Kelley, Reprints of Economic Classics, 1969, pp. 87-98 and 160-205.

[36] Heaton, H., *A Scholar in Action Edwin F. Gay*, Cambridge, Mass. Harvard University Press, 1952, p. 30.

[37] The above data was taken from Farnam, H. W., op.cit., pp. 25-27.

and economics students returned with German degrees. What is important to keep in mind is that, as Farnam confessed, his years in Germany had opened up for him an entirely new world.[38]

Young American would-be economists and would-be historians were favorably impressed with the way in which social sciences were taught in Germany. In addition to the above-mentioned scope of German academic freedom, history and economics enjoyed considerably more public attention there than in America. Furthermore, the study of history and economics commanded considerable popular respect as well.[39]

More than twenty years ago, Professor Herbst, in an attempt to evaluate the impact of the transfer of German culture to the United States around the turn of the century, wrote that American students in Germany were "the more impressed by the doctrines of German historians concerning the relation of history to politics in the years immediately following the crisis of the Civil War, when many American students saw in Prussia's rise to national leadership a parallel to the victory of the North in that conflict."[40]

For American economists, the education and training of Richard T. Ely is very instructive in grasping the transfer of German New Economics to America in the second half of the 19th century. Ely sailed for Germany in May of 1877.[41] Upon arrival, he spent a summer learning the German language in Kiel, and then proceeded to the university of Halle, where he met a fellow American, Simon N. Patten, the future professor of economics at the University of Pennsylvania, of Philadelphia, Pennsylvania.[42] In Halle, Ely also met Edmund J. James and Joseph French Johnson, Americans who became prominent academics later on.

While at Halle, the young Ely met and worked under Professor Johannes Conrad, who was chiefly interested in problems of agrarian policy and agricultural statistics.[43] Conrad was the well-known author of a textbook in economics, known as *Grundriss der politischen Ökonomie*, which in 1923 was in its 11th edition. In the spring of 1878, Ely went to the University of Heidelberg, where he became a student of Karl Knies and Johann K. Bluntschli. Karl Knies became Ely's "Master," and Knies' idea that economics belongs "neither to the natural nor to the mental sciences, but to the group of historical disciplines which have for their object the study of man in society in terms of its historical growth" left an indelible impression on Ely.[44] Knies was also quite sympathetic to the

---

[38] Farnam, H. W., *ibid.*, p. 27.

[39] For a few salient facts on the social studies in Germany after the mid-19th century, see, Paulsen F., *The German Universities and University Study*, New York, Charles Scribner's Sons, 1906, pp. 243-262.

[40] Herbst, J., *op.cit.*, p. 112.

[41] Ely, R. T., *Ground Under Our Feet*, New York, The Macmillan Co., 1938, p. 37.

[42] *Ibid.*, p. 38.

[43] *Ibid.*, p. 40.

aspirations of the German working man as was Bluntschli, whose favorite phrase was that working people deserve "an existence worthy of human being."[45] Ely took his Ph. D. in economics *summa cum laude* in 1879.[46] Upon graduation, he went to Berlin, where he worked with the Director of the Prussian Statistical Bureau, Dr. Ernst Engel, and with Professor Adolph Wagner.[47] Ely returned to New York in 1880.

Ely had sailed to Germany in quest of truth in the field of economics. He thought he had found it in the German universities, and he wanted to put it to good use in his native country. But upon his return to New York City in mid-summer of 1880, Dr. Ely was out of work. As he walked the streets in search of a job, he saw "dirty," treeless streets. On every side evidence of ugly corruption, of municipal incompetence, of an improper conception of the role of government met his sensitive eyes ... Nostalgia, a momentary desire to return to Europe, the Europe which had opened his eyes to a brave new world that lay ahead, welled up within him.[48] At that moment, he resolved to help the underprivileged underdogs in America.

According to Ely, the year of 1876, when the United States was celebrating its first centennial, actually heralded a new era in political economy.[49] In the meantime, Ely had joined the faculty of Johns Hopkins University in Baltimore as a lecturer in political economy; there, in 1887, he was promoted to the rank of associate professor.[50] At Johns Hopkins, Ely quickly became a leader of "new economics," something that he had brought across the Atlantic from Germany. In essence, Ely's "new economics" amounted to hostility to the classical highly deductive school of economics. Ely admitted that the British classical school of economics was attractive because of its 'enticing unity and alluring simplicity.'[51] But it failed as a guide in real life, and its "laissez-faire, laissez-passer" amounted to a complete social fiasco; in Ely's view, classical economics was good for 'academics only.'[52] It had no real appreciation for the public good and its pre-occupation with individual self-interest neglected social considerations.[53]

---

[44] *Ibid.*, p. 44.

[45] *Ibid.*, p. 45.

[46] Schlabach, T. F., "Ely, Richard Theodore, April 13, 1854-October 4, 1943," in *Dictionary of American Biography*, Supplement # 3 (1941-1945), New York, Scribner's 1973, pp. 248-251.

[47] *Ibid.*, p. 51.

[48] Rader, B. G., *The Academic Mind and Reform. The Influence of Richard T. Ely in American Life*, Lexington, Kentucky, University of Kentucky Press, 1966, p. 1.

[49] Ely, R. T., "The Past and Present of Political Economy," in *Johns Hopkins University Studies in Historical and Political Science*, vol. 2, 1884.

[50] Schlabach, T. F., *op.cit.*, p. 248.

[51] Ely, R. T., *op.cit.*, p. 17.

[52] *Ibid.*, p. 24.

[53] *Ibid.*, p. 36.

As a student of Conrad and Knies, Ely had become convinced that history, experience, and statistical methods had become indispensable tools of economic inquiry.[54] He acquired a strong dislike for the "absolutism of economic theory" and he cast aside all *a priori* doctrines of economics. Ely also emphasized that when German economists noticed social evils "they did not hesitate to counsel" government officials.[55] German economists, popularly known as German Historical Economists, strove to develop economics on an "inductive basis."[56] They were also members of the *Verein für Socialpolitik* who eagerly collected statistical data for social legislation that was needed to prevent the drift of the industrial masses into he hands of Marxists. Ely's teachers were not socialists, but reformers, who strove to undo the social evils of unrestrained laissez-faire.[57]

Ely's teacher at the University of Halle, Johannes Conrad, urged the American students attending his seminar to set up an American counterpart of the *Verein für Socialpolitik* upon return to the United States, if you "were to have any influence whatever upon the course of practical politics."[58] Conrad felt that Americans must take a new attitude toward the whole subject of social legislation. The young Americans were thus imbued with a legislative zeal designed to cope with the excesses of unfettered laissez-faire, exploitative, monopolistic practices, absence of meaningful collective bargaining in the industrial sector, and the lack of labor unions, slum-clearance programs, social security of any kind, maternity leaves, health insurance, and unemployment compensation. All of the above legislation had been passed in Germany in the decade of the 1880s. Germany had retained a viable market economy and parliamentary democracy, and Germans had retained private ownership of the means of production in industry and agriculture.

With such ideas in mind, and, united in their rejection of laissez-faire economics, the young American Turks—Adams, Clark, Patten, Seligman, and Ely—founded the American Economic Association in 1885.[59] The creation of the Association was a stormy affair, to say the least, as Professor A. W. Coats has noted.[60] These German-educated economists were rebels within the economics profession united against laissez-faire and classical orthodoxy. They were depressed "with the sterility of the old economics which was being taught in the American colleges."[61] Ely also wrote in his memoirs that he and the other young

---

[54] *Ibid.*, pp. 43-45.

[55] *Ibid.*, p. 49.

[56] Dorfman, J., *op.cit.*, p. 18.

[57] *Ibid.*, p. 20.

[58] Ely, R. R., *Ground Under Our Feet*, New York, The Macmillan Co., 1938, p. 134.

[59] *Ibid.*, p. 121.

[60] Coats, A. W., "The American Economic Association and the Economics Profession," in *Journal of Economic Literature*, vol. 23, #4, 1985, pp. 1697-1727.

[61] Ely, R. T., *op.cit.*, p. 132.

American Turks had tried to set up an organization which would have borne the name of the *Society for the Study of National Economy*, sponsored by Simon N. Patten and Edmund J. James.[62] It would have been almost a replica of the German *Verein für Socialpolitik*. The conservatives within the profession, however, ably supported by "moneys bags" sitting on the boards of trustees of American Ivy-League universities slowly, brutally, and mercilessly brought this group of German-educated heretics to their knees.

Who were the most respresentative of these German-bred social scientists? Dorfman, in his short article of 1955, singled out five American social scientists: John B. Clark, Edmund J. James, Richard T. Ely, Henry C. Adams, and Edwin R. A. Seligman.[63] One could easily add a few more individuals who played an important role in the evolution of the American Institutionalist School of Economics around the turn of the 20th century. One was Simon Nelson Patten, who met Ely at the University of Halle, and who taught at the University of Pennsylvania from 1888 to his retirement in 1916.[64] German-educated, Patten's brand of economics was heresy in America at that time. But he persisted, and published his first book, *The Premises of Political Economy*, in 1885. In the course of his thirty years at the University of Pennsylvania, Patten published 20 books and more than 100 articles and essays. His *New Basis for Civilization*, published between 1907 and 1921, was his most popular work. He was a much admired and inspiring teacher.[65] Patten was not a classroom economist, because he often suggested that the "place of the economist is on the firing line of civilization."[66] His economics, in essence, was a revolt against classical economic theories. He favored social legislation along the lines of the early German welfare economists, popularly known as German Historical economists. His best known disciple was Rexford Tugwell, who became influential under President Roosevelt in the 1930s, and who exerted considerable legislative influence under the New Deal.[67]

In his lifetime, Patten was much read, but, because of the prevailing conditions of laissez-faire in America, much misunderstood. As noted in the history of the University of Pennsylvania, "his economic theories were in advance of his time, and the implications of those theories were frequently obscured by the variety of means he proposed in the hope of realizing an economy of abundance more

---

[62] *Ibid.*, p. 133.

[63] Dorfman, J., "The Role of the German Historical School in American Economic Thought," in *American Economic Review*, vol. 45, 1955, pp. 23-27.

[64] Meyerson, M. and Winegard, D. P., *Gladly Learn and Gladly Teach. Franklin and his Heirs at the University of Pennsylvania, 1740-1976*, Philadelphia, Pa., University of Pennsylvania Press, 1978, especially chapter 12, called Simon Nelson Patten: Economics and Social Thought in the Wharton School, pp. 145-155.

[65] Nearing, S., "A Prince Among Paupers," in *Great Teachers Portrayed by Those Who Studied Under Them*, edited by Peterson, H., New Brunswick, Rutgers University Press, 1946, pp. 155-170.

[66] Meyerson, M. and Winegard, D. P., *op.cit.*, p. 148.

[67] *Ibid.*, p. 153.

rapidly."[68] Patten heralded the economic and social developments of the New Deal, something he clearly picked up in Bismarck's Germany of the 1880s. Another German-trained American economist was Edwin F. Gay (1867-1946).[69] In 1890, he sailed for Europe where he spent twelve and a half years, studying history and social sciences at various universities, learning languages, and doing research.[70] In 1891, Gay went to Berlin, and in 1893 turned to the serious study of political economy and took courses with Adolph Wagner and Gustav Schmoller.[71]

Wagner impressed the young Gay with a number of important ideas and concepts. For instance, Wagner insisted that Christian ethics must govern economic behavior. He denounced the doctrine of "untrammelled individualism" as often being unethical. He said government should protect the economically weak, poorly-paid, and disadvantaged segments of society. And he called on economists to use their influence to persuade legislators to pass wise and good laws—laws to regulate natural monopolies, for instance, and laws to allow the operation of public enterprises in certain sectors of the economy. Gay admitted that he was very much attracted to this interventionist creed of Wagner.[72] But it was Schmoller who really fired up Gay and touched off his interest and enthusiasm for the "new" German economics. Schmoller taught Gay that "economics could be brought into close interrelation with psychology, ethics, history, and political science to produce a real science of society."[73] That is, in economics, one explores not only the relationships between man and material goods, but also among men. Furthermore, economic phenomena are an inextricable part of social life and must be always evaluated from an ethical point of view.

The second reason for Gay's attraction to Schmoller's work was Schmoller's concern for social betterment of the masses and his desire to create "a science of economics which would serve as a sure guide for policies of social betterment."[74] Schmoller disdained the speculative assumptions of the classical economists. He turned to the study of history, the study of institutions and their evolution, and the study of social statistics to make economics an inductive science that was realistic and factual. During his lifetime, Schmoller insisted that economists must learn all the history they can in order to have a solid ground under their feet. Once they have it, general principles are likely to emerge, and

---

[68] *Ibid.*, p. 155.

[69] Hamilton, E. J., "Gay, Edwin Francis (October 27, 1867-February 8, 1946)" in *Dictionary of American Biography, Supplement # 4, 1946-1950*, New York, Scribner's, 1974, pp. 321-322.

[70] Heaton, H., *A Scholar in Action. Edwin F. Gay*, Cambridge, Mass., Harvard University Press, 1952, p. 30.

[71] *Ibid.*, p. 38.

[72] *Ibid.*, p. 38.

[73] *Loc. cit.*

[74] *Ibid.*, p. 39.

economists can effectively lobby legislators, government officials, etc. Economics for Schmoller was not a science for the classroom only. Gay found Schmoller in his seminar to be "calm, judical, slow of speech, methodically proceeding step by step, convincing by the completeness of his treatment, yet tolerant and humble."[75]

Gay wrote his dissertation under Schmoller on the English enclosure movement and earned his doctorate in 1902 with highest honors from the University of Berlin.[76] Gay's biographer wrote later that his long years in Europe "had permitted his scholarship to become wide and deep,"[77] and that Gay had given "much thought to the interrelations among history, economics, politics, religion, and philosophy; and had developed a discriminating taste in literature, music, and the arts."[78]

Yet Earl J. Hamilton, in his biographical sketch of Gay was of contrary opinion. He wrote that the "chief weakness of Gay's German training was the lack of rigorous instruction in economic analysis—squeezed out of German universities in his day by historicism—as a result of which he never fully understood the self-regulating functions of a free market economy."[79] Regardless of this supposedly inadequate academic preparation, Gay taught at Harvard from 1902 to 1917 and from 1924 to 1936, when he retired. He was a great teacher and a man of remarkable administrative ability. During World War I, he left Harvard and served with distinction on the United States Shipping Board. In fact, his work in Washington, D.C. earned him a reputation as one of the "miracle men" of the war.[80] Gay also directed the government's Central Bureau of Planning and Statistics, which was set up in June 1918. In 1919, he was a founder fo the *National Bureau of Economic Research* and served as its first president. Gay was also responsible for the establishment of *Foreign Affairs*. In 1929, he served as president of the *American Economic Association* and in 1940 he was the first president of the *Economic History Association*.

As Gay became an influential force on the American intellectual scene, he radiated his German scholarship all over the country. He was particularly successful in stressing the significance of the "contiguous fields" surrounding the core of economics. He was not interested in speculative economic theory. Today, American economists do not even know his name. Those who do, would dub him an economic historian. And economic history today, among economic theorists, either counts for nothing or is considered a characteristic of professional incompetence.

---

[75] *Ibid.*, p. 39.

[76] *Ibid.*, pp. 56-57.

[77] *Ibid.*, p. 57.

[78] *Loc. cit.*

[79] *Dictionary of American Biography, Supplement # 4, 1946-1950*, New York, Scribner's, 1974, p. 321.

[80] Hamilton, E. H., *ibid.*, p. 322.

Another German-trained scholar, Albion Woodbury Small (May 11, 1854 - March 24, 1926), is also virtually unknown today by American economists. But he left an indelible mark on the emergence of sociology in the United States.[81] Upon graduation from Colby College, Small entered Newton Theological Institution, from which he graduated in 1879. Soon thereafter, he left for Germany where he spent two years studying political economy and history at the Universities of Leipzig and Berlin.[82] He returned to America in 1881 with a German wife and "a set of German ideas which would be his stock in trade throughout his acdemic career."[83]

From 1881 to 1889, Small taught at Colby College. In 1889, he took the Ph. D. degree from Johns Hopkins University, where some of his fellow-students were John R. Commons, Woodrow Wilson, and Frederick Jackson Turner. While at Johns Hopkins, Small came under the spell of Richard T. Ely, who was teaching there then. Upon graduation, Small was appointed president of Colby College. In 1892, Small, then thirty-eight years old, was invited to set up a new department of social science at the University of Chicago. Thorstein Veblen was also brought to Chicago at the same time. The sociology department Small set up was "the first department of its kind in the U.S."[84] He remained at Chicago for the rest of his life, retiring in 1924. He founded the *American Journal of Sociology*, edited and contributed prolifically to it from 1895 to 1926. In 1890, Small published his *Introduction to a Science of Society*, followed by his *General Sociology*. He published *Adam Smith and Modern Sociology* in 1907, and followed it with *The Cameralists*, probably his most important contribution to economic thought, in 1909. Small's *The Meaning of Social Science* appeared in 1910, and in 1913 came *Between Eras: from Capitalism to Democracy*, Small's powerful indictment of the laissez-faire type capitalist system.

For Albion W. Small, the field of sociology was not for the classroom. He made no bones of the fact that "the roots of the true path to scientific knowledge of society were in Germany."[85] All his life, Small strove to have an impact upon contemporary events. He despised ivory-tower academia and academics.[86] For Small, the study of sociology was first and foremost a means of gaining the knowledge needed for social reforms. He advocated social engineering and proper legislation on the basis of the accepted social theory of his day.[87] Obviously Small was very much influenced by the work of the *Verein für Socialpolitik* in Germany. In fact, Small's biographer felt that Small was a

---

[81] E. F., Small, "Albion Woodbury (May 11, 1854 - March 1926)," in *Dictionary of American Biography*, New York, Scribner's, pp. 221 - 222.

[82] Christakes, G., *Albion W. Small*, Boston, Twayne Publishers, 1978, p. 17.

[83] *Ibid.*, p. 18.

[84] E. F., *op.cit.*, p. 221.

[85] Christakes, G., *op.cit.*, p. 23.

[86] *Ibid.*, p. 25.

[87] *Ibid.*, p. 34.

conduit through which many European ideas—particularly German—were introduced into this country.[88]

But the very idea of social legislation, designed to improve the lot of industrial workers, permit the formation of labor unions, legitimize their work and prescribe work rules, health codes, health, accident, and maternity insurance, and unemployment compensation, was a near-heresy in America of 1890. Laissez-faire was still the order of the day in the economic arrangements in this country.[89] Ideas of social control and suggestions for welfare legislation for industrial workers were repulsive, both to the American public and to many tune-calling social scientists. All German-trained and educated social scientists—historians, economists, and political scientists—had to learn the hard way that German welfare legislation of the 1880s was acceptable in Germany, but not in the United States. Interferences of this kind were dubbed socialistic or anarchistic.

Small influenced many social scientists, like John Dewey, Judge Brandeis, Walter Lippmann and Judge Holmes, but economists today have no idea who he was. And yet sociology is an indispensable "contiguous" field, surrounding the core of economics. A search of the *Dictionary of American Biography*, turns up many other German-trained Americans, including Arthur Twining Hadley (1856-1930), Charles William Macfarlane (1850-1931), Henry Rogers Seager (1870-1930), Frank William Taussig (1859-1940), Frank Albert Fetter (1863-1949), Charles Richmond Henderson (1848-1915), Abram Piatt Andrew (1873-1936), Winthrop More Daniels (1867-1944), and Roland Post Falkner (1866-1940). These and many others made contributions to American scholarship in the fields of history, sociology, economics, theology. Out of this broad-based German economics tradition eventually emerged the Institutional School of Economics.

When they returned to America, many of the German-trained and educated young scholars experienced considerable difficulty in readjusting. There were a number of reasons for this. For one, in Germany they had gotten used to the idea that in the States they would enjoy academic freedom comparable to the *Lehrfreiheit and Lernfreiheit* (freedom of research and instruction) they had known in Germany. Alas, they were taught an unpleasant, severe lesson soon enough. Richard T. Ely, for instance, was in the eyes of J. Franklin Jameson, a German-trained American, "infatuated with the German Historical School of Economics."[90] In no time at all, Ely's view of what the Federal government should do brought him into conflict with his university, the American business community, and the mass media. In his celebrated *Outlines of Economics*, he

---

[88] *Ibid.,* p. 1.

[89] Higgs, R., *Crisis and Leviathan. Critical Episodes in the Growth of American Government,* New York, Oxford University Press, 1987, p. 4, 22, and pp. 77-105.

[90] Rader, B. G., *The Academic Mind and Reform. The Influence of Richard T. Ely in American Life,* Lexington, Kentucky, University of Kentucky Press, 1966, p. 20.

entitled part VI, "The Relation of the State to Industry,"[91] and offered a long list of the government's duties. His suggestions resembled those of Schmoller and the *Verein für Socialpolitik*. In 1894, after his move to the University of Wisconsin Ely was put on trial on the basis of trumped-up charges of "economic heresy."[92] He was accused by Oliver E. Wells, Wisconsin's superintendent of public instruction, of having propagated at the university socialist principles, even though he had masked them as something else. In an article in the widely read periodical, *Nation*, Wells said Ely was "guilty of teaching and practicing heretical economic doctrines."[93] Wells accused the professor of advocating utopian, pernicious doctrines that supposedly justified attacks on life and property. Besides being a bleeding-heart who took the cause of the poor people, Ely was an organizer of labor unions, Wells said.[94] Ely was completely vindicated at his trial and it was established once and for all that he was not a dangerous Marxist socialist. This must have been small comfort to the professor. After all, he was the most widely read economist in the United States up to 1893, according to Rader. Ely was indeed an advocate of reforms, but he also believed in private property of the means of production. He tempered this belief, however, by advocating government restrictions and controls on some natural monopolies. He defended the Constitution and the democratic form of government, and was an advocate of a market economy. From today's perspective, he was an advocate of Germany-style welfare legislation of the 1880s. He wanted to introduce some measure of protection for the little men by way of medical, health, and unemployment insurance. Ely was not fired from his post at the University of Wisconsin and he achieved complete vindication.[95]

Others were not so lucky. Many unorthodox economics professors were simply fired from their posts. John R. Commons was so dismissed and so was Edward H. Bemis from the University of Chicago.[96] Being an economic heretic or even an apostate in an environment of laissez-faire, where businessmen controlled the boards of trustees of private universities, was not easy in those days.

---

[91] New York, The Macmillan Company, 1912, revised and enlarged edition, pp. 458-470. See also his "Certain Psychological Phases of Industrial Evolution," in *Congress of Arts and Science, Universal Exposition, St. Louis, 1904*, edited by Rogers, H. J., vol. 7, Boston and New York, Houghton Mifflin, 1906, pp. 807-813.

[92] "Professor Ely Charged with Economic Heresy," in *Public Opinion*, vol. 17, August 16, 1894, pp. 462-463.

[93] Rader, B. G., *op.cit.*, p. 130.

[94] Ely, R. T., *Ground Under Our Feet*, New York, The Macmillan Company, 1938, pp. 219-221.

[95] "The Trial of Professor Ely," in *The Dial*, vol. 17, 1894, pp. 109-110. See also, Ely, R. T., *Ground Under our Feet*, p. 232.

[96] *Public Opinion*, vol. 19, 1895, pp. 296-297 contains many excerpts from numerous newspapers, which castigated the 'money power' and the necessity of freedom of research in American universities.

Another difficult adjustment for German-bred social scientists was to return from the elitist, intellectual milieu of Europe to populist America. In America, people participated in the political process as free citizens, whereas in Germany university professors became part of the democratic process through their official status as professional specialists.[97] This difference imposed many obstacles on returning American scholars. But social scientists may have found the transition even harder. While in Germany and other European countries, the young Americans may have picked up the race theories ubiquitous at that time. Herbst in his volume alluded to this problem,[98] but did not explore it. An example of this racist tainting was John Burgess,[99] who spent a semester at the University of Göttingen.[100] Burgess once wrote that in selecting immigrants, America must "preserve our Aryan nationality in the State, and admit to its membership only such non-Aryan race-elements as shall have become Aryanized in spirit and in genius by contact with it."[101] Furthermore, in 1907 in Berlin, Burgess characterized Slavs, Czechs, Hungarians, and South Italians as 'rabble' that Uncle Sam does not want for citizens.[102]

What were the race theories of 19th-century Europe? In addition to anti-Jewish legislation of the Christian Church, all European nations, including Germany, had developed their own brands of Judaeophobia. In Germany, it manifested itself in the form of Volkish ideology, and was based on the medieval notion that the Jew was an alien in the land of the Germanic peoples. According to popular stereotypes, Jews were dishonest, ruthless, and consumed with a lust for power. They could not be trusted because they practiced "a subversion from within." The Church's teachings about Jews were far more influential than anti-Jewish legislation. Anti-Jewish 'pictorial' representation in Church sculpture and stained-glass windows and anti-Jewish teaching in regular Sunday sermons reached millions and were potent not only in Europe but also in England, in the United States, and Orthodox Tsarist Russia.

In the second half of the 19th century, these popular stereotypes were transformed and given pseudo-scientific trappings.[103] The Frenchman Count Joseph Arthur de Gobineau was probably the first modern race theorist. His work, *The Inequality of Human Races*, published in 1853, is a comprehensive

---

[97] Herbst, J., *op.cit.*, p. 112.

[98] Herbst, H., *ibid.*, pp. 122-123.

[99] Burgess, J., *Uncle Sam. Reminiscences of an American Scholar*, New York, 1937.

[100] Buchloh, P. G. and Rix W. T., *American Colony of Göttingen. Historical and Other Data Collected Between the Years 1855 and 1888*, Göttingen, Vandenhoeck and Ruprecht, 1976, p. 45.

[101] Quoted by Herbst, H., *op.cit.*, p. 122.

[102] *Loc.cit.*

[103] For a discussion of the various race theories, see Balabkins, N., *West German Reparations to Israel*, New Brunswick, N. J., Rutgers University Press, 1971, especially chapter, called "Germany's Road into Industrial Genocide," pp. 3-18.

exposition of white supremacy, and in his writings the concept of race becomes the focus for all human history. Gobineau was largely ignored by the French, but his influence was strong among German teachers, in the grade and high school levels, "who were in a position to disseminate the racist ideas on the schools."[104]

Another writer whose work on the racial question had immense influence on the European masses was Houston Stewart Chamberlain, a naturalized German of English parentage and birth. He combined the theories of Gobineau with Nietzsche's concept of the superman, and this aggregation, with his additions, resulted in his *The Foundations of the Nineteenth Century*, published in 1899. This pseudo-scientific tract preached Teutonic racial superiority, and became, over time, the Bible of anti-Jewish academics and Jew-baiting, Volkish ideologists.

The next major work in this genre was the two-volume work by the Frenchman Edward Dromont. His *La France Juive*, published in 1886, charged that Jews had been responsible for French woes since the Middle Ages. In this work, the Jew emerges as the eternal conspirator-felon, the pariah of nations. The diabolical Jew, a man of superior cunning, was denounced as the real enemy of all people.

Americans studying at European universities heard all these pseudo-scientific race theories as well as the popular slogans of the Jew-baiters. How much of all this negative pseudo-learning returned to America is hard to measure, but, undeniably, some of it did. Only the shock of the Nazi Genocide of European Jewry during World War II destroyed most of this 19th century European pseudo-learning in America. The aftermath of this industrial genocide by the Nazis slowly led to a remarkable and worldwide modification of Christian attitudes towards Jews. The former hostility is largely gone today, at least in socially sanctioned terms.

Schmoller was not oblivious to this important question, which he discussed in his *Grundriss*, vol. I, in a section called "Races and Nations" (Die Rassen und Völker). To introduce properly the subject matter, Schmoller, with typical thoroughness, cited works by 32 authors from such diverse fields as anthropology, geography, biology, natural inheritance, political anthropology, general anthropology, and ethnography. He also cited W. D. Babington's *Fallacies of Race Theories as Applied to National Characteristics*. According to Schmoller, climate, living conditions, and the mingling of races accounted for the emergence of different nations and different racial features over the millenia. On pp. 149-150, he referred specifically to the Jewish population in Germany, and said that to judge the beneficial impact of the Jewish people in Germany or any other country, one had to consider their numbers, their social position, and their trades. Schmoller was particularly fond of the fact that Jewish business people

---

[104] Mosse, G. L., *The Crisis of German Ideology*, New York, Grosset and Dunlap, 1964, p. 91.

increased the level of competition in the market place (p. 150). On the other hand, he deplored Jewish businessmen for exploiting poor peasants and poor workers (p. 150), but Schmoller appreciated the remarkable integration of German Jews into the mainstream of German society, and, on p. 150, he wrote that it was simply wrong to condemn the mingling of different races.

Schmoller himself was never either a philo-Semite or anti-Semite.[105] Yet at the very end of his life, in 1917, he was obliged to bare his breast on this question. In a short article, he expounded on his life-long method of evaluating the contri- bution of Jews both to German society and economy and to the societies and economies of other countries. He first asked the following questions: How many Jews had a university education? How large were the Jewish middle class and the Jewish working class? What was the spatial distribution of Jews in a particular country? Finally, how high was the cultural and political niveau of the country in which the Jews lived?

Since the period between 1848 and 1870, Germany had made great strides in assimilating the Jewish upper classes. But the process had not been completed, even at the time Schmoller wrote this article. He noted that the presence of 615,021 Jews among 60 million Germans could not be objectionable.[106] The assimilation of Jews, in Schmoller's mind, had been a "happy addition to the German race."[107] He knew well that German Jews had encountered bigotry and barriers to certain professions, but Schmoller was aware that century-long prejudices die slowly and cannot be changed overnight. In conclusion, Schmoller was an accomplished and much respected social scientist of the late 19th century who problably had individual likes and dislikes, but who did not condemn anyone simply because he was Jewish.

Apart from this rather questionable cultural import, what distinguished virtually all of the more than 9,000 young Americans who had studied in Germany prior to World War I was their knowledge of the German and French languages. Unlike today, when most American academics are monolingual,[108] economists, historians, and social scientists of three generations ago read and wrote in many European languages. A cursory glance at the *American Journal of Sociology* and the *Political Science Quarterly* reveals an exciting interaction among scholary communities across the ocean. Social scientists, broad-based as they were, were familiar with many contiguous fields of knowledge surrounding the core of economics.

Alas, the deplorable linguistic deficiency among American economists today deprives them of the ability to learn from other economists. The only new

---

[105] Schmoller, G., "Die heutige Judenfrage," in *Zwanzig Jahre Deutscher Politik*, München, Duncker & Humblot, 1920, p. 12.

[106] *Ibid.*, p. 179.

[107] *Ibid.*, p. 179.

[108] Simon, P., *The Tongue-Tied American. Confronting the Foreign Language Crisis*, New York, Centinuum, 1980, pp. 102-122.

language that American economists have acquired since 1920 is mathematics, and today, indeed, they communicate in Greek symbols. Since the end of World War II, Americans have assumed that a knowledge of English was enough by itself to solve all problems. Now, when Americans step on foreign soil, they expect to speak English. American academics assume that they can deliver their material anywhere in the world in English.

As noted above, German-trained and educated Americans had a difficult time transplanting to American soil the "welfare economics" they brought back from Germany. But their excellent linguistic skills contributed substantially to the transplantation to America of much of the spiritual treasures of the European Renaissance, Reformation, and the Enlightenment.

The specific and lasting contribution of the intensive interaction between America and Germany prior to World War I was in the field of American higher education. Up to the mid-1850s, graduate schools did not exist in this country, which was one reason so many young Americans went to Europe. In the 1870s, American launched a vigorous reform of higher education and German-style graduate schools emerged.[109] The German university, with its *Lehrfreiheit and Lernfreiheit*, became a mold for American reformers, who proceeded to incorporate many German features into American higher education.[110]

Surely, the most tangible influence of Wilhelm Roscher, Bruno Hildebrand, Karl Knies, Gustav Schmoller, Johannes Conrad, and others was on the American Institutionalist School of Economics. The contributions of Thorstein Veblen, John R. Commons, Wesley C. Mitchell, John M. Clark, Rexford G. Tugwell, Gardiner C. Means, Clarence E. Ayres, John Kenneth Galbraith, and others are well-known.[111] Their work was primarily concerned with the German intellectual departures in economic thought that led to the assault on laissez-faire. The German economists made a valiant attempt to retain a market economy, while protecting the weaker segments of the population from the strong and greedy. They wanted to retain private ownership of the means of production in industry and agriculture, while introducing the measures known today as a "welfare net": unemployment compensation, health and accident insurance, and other employment benefits.

The "older" group of German critics of laissez-faire and the "younger" group, led by Schmoller, liked and defended a multi-party political system. Schmoller remained a monarchist. Up to World War I, monarchies prevailed in England, Germany, Italy, Austria-Hungary, and the Low Countries.

---

[109] Ely, T. R., "American College and German Universities," in *Early Reform in American Higher Education*, Chicago, Nelson-Hall Company, 1972, pp. 77-91.

[110] Veysey, L. R., *The Emergence of the American University*, Chicago, The University of Chicago Press, 1965, pp. 125-133, and pp. 263-268.

[111] n.a., *Institutional Economics. Veblen, Commons, and Mitchell Reconsidered*, Berkeley and Los Angeles, University of California Press, 1963, 183 pp.

The members of the *Verein für Socialpolitik* were broad-based economists who studied all the areas contiguous to economics, The same was true for the American Institutionalists. In America, the law schools slowly became the training grounds for civil servants. The rising of American schools of business emerged as places where business executives received their training. In both types of institutions the broad-based method of instruction is the rule, even though no one remembers that it was developed by the German economists in the last century and brought over to this country.

Thousands of Americans had earned their degrees in Germany prior to World War I, including hundreds in the social sciences and economics. But their impact on U. S. thought, in Schmoller's view, was mixed. Writing in 1911, he felt that two major schools of economics had emerged in the United States: a theoretical one, linking up with the former English classical school and incorporating elements of the Austrian School of Economics; and the realistic school, which was influenced by German economists. Schmoller felt that the high intellectual niveau of the New England states favored abstract modes of thinking, but that such a manner of thinking would produce "unrealistic, purely abstract literature." The main representatives of this school of thought were John B. Clark, Simon Patten, Frank Fetter, Irving Fischer, Edwin Seligman, and John Commons, among many others. Clark, the leader of this group, was a first-class scientist, but, in Schmoller's view, his work was "Ivory Towerish" (weltabgewandt).[112] Schmoller went on to say that there was little agreement among abstract American economic theorists. As he put it, there was almost "infinite amount of sagacity, plenty of good ideas, speculation, but also a confusing diversity."[113] The theorists, Schmoller said, were engaging in "wholesome intellectual gymnastics" but sooner or later they would have to make a realistic examination of their "unrealistic premises."[114]

The second American school of economics, Schmoller felt, was realistic and sober, and kept a proper distance from all socialistic ideas, thanks to the influence of German training. Schmoller was particularly happy about the emergence of the American statistical tradition, which, he felt, would eventually overshadow the purely speculative branch of American economics.[115]

Alas, Schmoller was wrong in this prediction. The Ivy-League universities of the American Northeast continue to practice extreme mathematization of economics even today. Of course, there are voices who urge the economics profession to return to the broad-based tradition of Gustav Schmoller.

---

[112] Schmoller, G., "Volkswirtschaft, Volkswirtschaftslehre und -methode," in *Handwörterbuch der Staatswissenschaften*, vol. 8, Jena, Gustav Fischer, 1911, p. 453.

[113] *Ibid.*, right isle, p. 453.

[114] *Ibid.*, p. 453.

[115] *Ibid.*, p. 454.

As we celebrate the sesquicentennial of his birth, maybe the mono-dimensional mathematical economists should at least acknowledge that economics is not just a classroom dicipline. Economists must help out legislators to prepare laws. To do that, they need some knowledge of economic history and institutional evolution and an awareness of social statistics. This was the real message of Schmoller. He did not study history and social statistics for their own sake. Modern economists surely have missed this aspect of Schmoller's message.

Concluding Observations on Schmoller's Legacy for the Economics Profession at the End of the Twentieth Century

Do Schmoller and his work have contemporary relevance? The answer is an unequivocal *yes*. But, this reaffirmation of Schmoller's importance is not a sentimental reflection on a German social scientist 150 years after his birth. Nor is it a predilection so typical of historians of economic thought to restore the intellectual fossils of yesteryear. Mainstream economists today virtually pruned the Schmollerian branch of economics from the family tree of economics. Consider, for example, Paul Samuelson's introductory textbook of economics. Since its first edition in 1948, it has been used by more than a million undergratuates. According to Samuelson's family tree of economics, the Classical School of Economics leads either to Marxist socialism or modern mainstream economics, via Neoclassical economics. The German Historical School of Economics is not even mentioned. Obviously, Samuelson assumes that it has contributed nothing to the evolution of economics in Western societies. Like an overzealous gardener, Samuelson has mistakenly identified Schmoller as deadwood and lopped him off the family tree of economics (see figure 1).

Samuelson thus makes no attempt to explain the rise of the contemporary Welfare State or, more narrowly, the origin of German Welfare Capitalism. As noted earlier in this volume, it was the German historical economists—Roscher, Hildebrand, Knies, Schmoller, and economists of the *Verein für Socialpolitik* —who argued that the accumulation of wealth in the hands of capitalists was by itself inadequate to fulfill the requirements of national well-being. The apalling social conditions of the working masses in English and German factory towns led these economists to realize that "do-nothing" or "do-very-little" government of laissez-faire was inadequate to create social harmony. The same conditions created an opportunity for Marxists who were already preaching open class warfare and who minced no words about their desire to overthrow the existing social order and replace it with the "dictatorship of the proletariat." Roscher, Hildebrand, and Knies said classical economics could not cape with the consequences of industrialization in Germany.

Roscher's solution to existing social ills was reform, not revolution. Hildebrand noted the deadly animosity and passionate class hatreds prevalent in England and Germany and pleaded for the reconciliation between capital and labor. To build solid foundations for future legislative reforms, Hildebrand

Figure 1

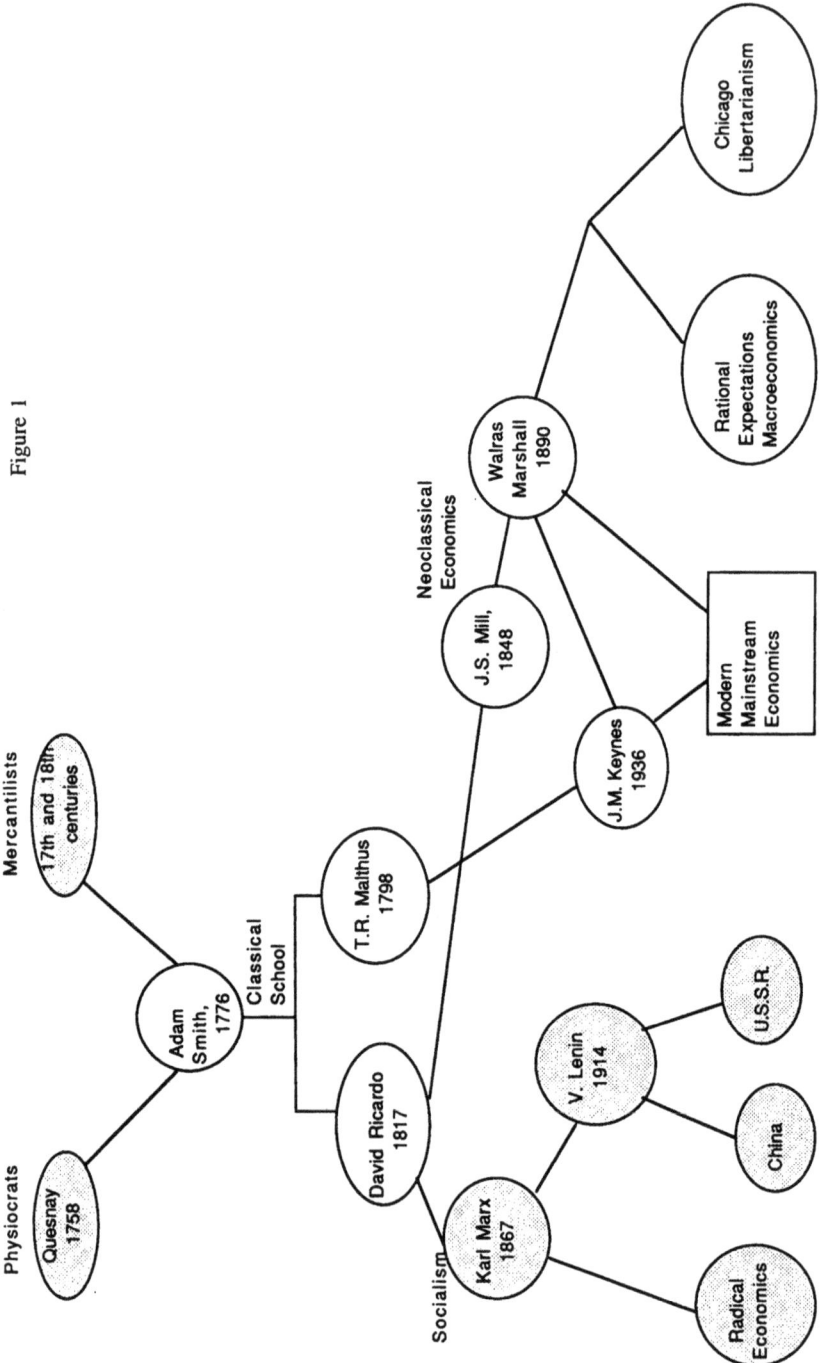

advocated careful and detailed monographs on social, institutional, and economic questions. Finally, Knies felt that the social ills spawned by laissez-faire actually amounted to a scientific justification of Marxist socialism, but he rejected the inevitability of socialism.

These three and other members of the early German Historical School of Economics wanted to modify the German social order and integrate the masses of the German workers into it. They were already thinking and writing in terms of a multi-dimensional social order or social space concept. Unfortunately, they had no organizational vehicle to press for social welfare legislation.

Gustav Schmoller was also horrified by the unintended social consequences of Germany's rapid industrialization. He knew of the violent uprising of the Silesian weavers of 1844 and he feared the spreading revolutionary fervor, particularly after 1848. Schmoller also dreaded the Marxist message and mission. But he also lacked a forum to conceive and advocate reforms.

Therefore, in 1872, Schmoller and others created the *Verein für Socialpolitik*, which advocated comprehensive welfare reform for the working masses. Under the leadership of Bismarck, the first welfare laws were passed in 1883 and *welfare capitalism* was launched. Schmoller's vision and forceful action played a major role in this effort. That is undeniably his legacy for posterity. But, alas, even today, more than one hundred years after the emergence of welfare capitalism, contemporary mainstream economists continue to take social systems for granted and relegate it to the *ceteris paribus* cage. Theoretical economists have become "social physicists" who regard social order matters as nothing but trivia!

But to Schmoller, social order matters were vital, and they inspired him for decades to fight against Marxist-led leftists and conservative-led reactionaries. Like John Maynard Keynes, Schmoller wanted to modify, stabilize and improve the social order and base it on a market economy, parliamentary democracy, and privately owned means of production. And yet, today, most economists are Keynesians, but nobody calls himself a Schmollerian.

In light of the above considerations, it is time to restore the missing Schmollerian branch to the family tree of economics, as presented below (figure 2).

The second major contribution of the German historical economists was an economic analysis method based not just on economic variables but on social factors as well. Karl Knies, who rejected the classical economists' method of isolating economic phenomena from social factors, may have inspired the late Swedish economist Gunnar Myrdal, who spoke often of such exclusion as the "illegitimate isolation." For Knies, such a method resembled "ripped-out eyes, which see nothing." Schmoller maintained that even the simplest economic phenomena did not lend themselves to purely deductive treatment. He frequently reminded economists that "circular causation" and "multiple causation" make the life of an economist difficult. Hence, to understand the

Figure 2

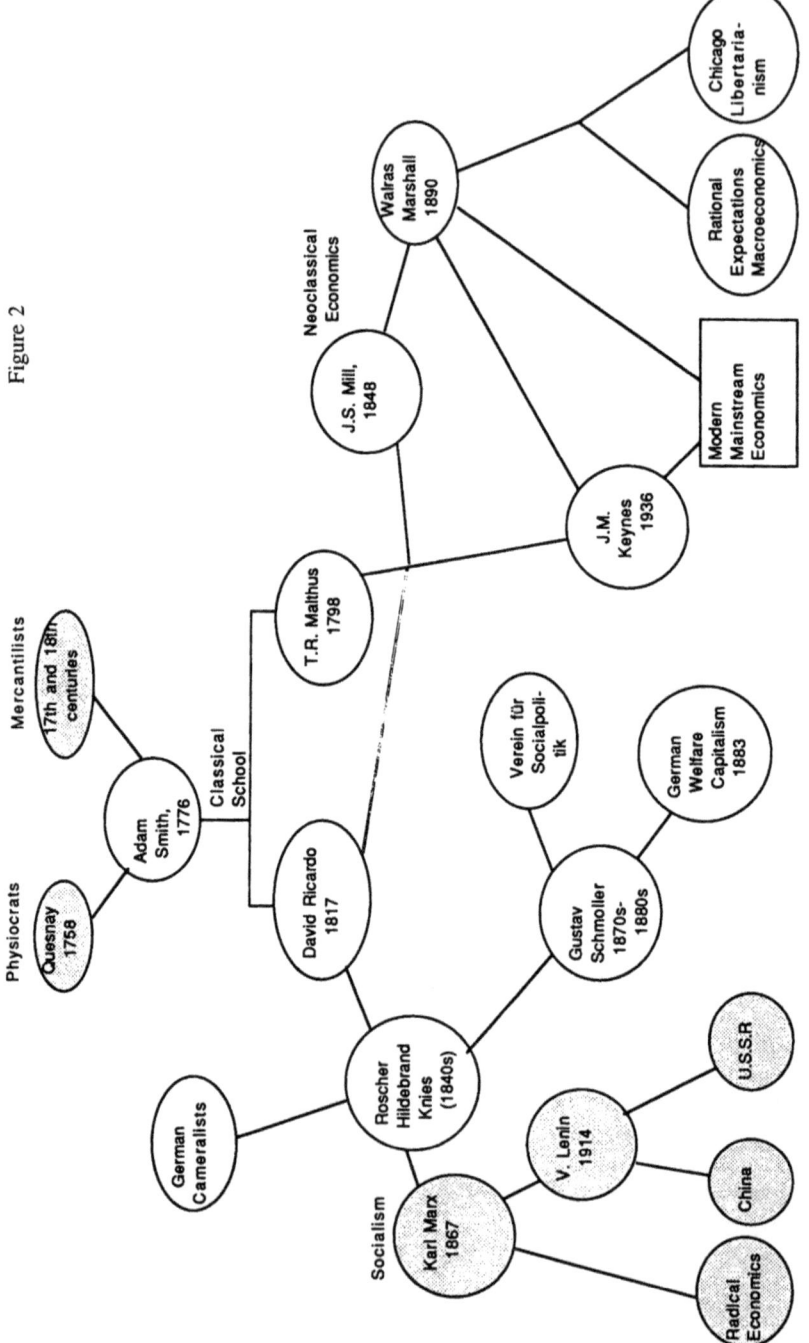

complexity of all social phenomena, Schmoller left for posterity his method of analysis. He believed that knowledge of economic history, statistics, institutions, economic theory, psychology, and technology would eventually lead to the emergence of the *Laws of Becoming* to supplement the classical *Laws of Being*. Schmoller obviously downplayed economic theory, but he cultivated what today is known as the *contiguous fields,* surrounding the core of economics. Schmoller also encouraged the training and education of broad-based men, who would become government officials, diplomats, teachers and academics. They would be jacks-of-many-trades and masters of none, but they would not become *idiots savants,* "brilliant at esoteric mathematics yet innocent of actual economic life," as John Kenneth Galbraith once wrote.[1]

Joseph A. Schumpeter and Myrdal also cultivated a broad-based method of scientific economic analysis, but neither left an appreciable mark on the mainstream economics of today. Nevertheless, despite the fads of the economics profession of today, economic policy-making will always require the knowledge of the contiguous fields. Schmoller's legacy may be largely overlooked today, but economists should at least be aware of why Schmoller urged them to be broadly educated. The tune-calling academic economists in America, for instance, continue to shine in the academic halls, but remain either oblivious or uninterested in the pressing social and economic problems of the day.

Finally, it is interesting to note that, despite contemporary ignorance of the German Historical School of Economics in general and Gustav Schmoller in particular, many, if not most, U. S. economists before World War I were German-educated. Almost 10,000 Americans studied at German universities and returned to this country with graduate degrees in chemistry, engineering, physics, as well as in economics and history. German-trained and educated economists founded the American Economic Association and laid the foundations for the American Institutional School of Economics.

The relentless flow of machinery, technology, scientific know-how, and trained manpower from Germany to the U. S. ended only with the outbreak of World War I, but not before it had contributed handsomely to the renaissance of America's intellectual life.

German-educated economists strove to re-orient the classical school of economics away from being an "armchair" or "classroom only" science. They strongly disliked equating economics with economic theory and they made no bones about it. They strove to produce a real science of society. They did not succeed, but they were responsible for setting up American graduate schools, and they contributed to the emergence of the American statistical tradition. The broad-based social science training that still goes on in the American law schools and schools of public administration is their forgotten legacy.

---

[1] Quoted in Colander, D. and Klamer, A. "The Making of an Economist," in *Economic Perspectives*, Vol. 1, No. 2, 1987, p. 95.

MIX
Papier aus verantwortungsvollen Quellen
Paper from responsible sources
FSC® C105338

Printed by Libri Plureos GmbH
in Hamburg, Germany